THE MAN JESUS

What You Need To Know About Jesus Christ

Ngozi Nwoke

PLASELDI LIMITED

NIGERIA

THE MAN JESUS

What You Need To Know About Jesus Christ

PLASEDI LIMITED
39 Yakubu Gowon Way,
Opp. Nitel, Jos, Plateau State,
Nigeria

Cover design by Wellington Kunaka

I appreciate all who contributed in one way or the other to my life and to this book. God bless you.

eBook ISBN **978-978-53766-4-7**

Table of Contents

Dedication

To the Father, the Son and the Holy Spirit who
gave the inspiration

Introduction

Jesus Christ. This name is so common that it has now become a household name in many parts of the world. Many call upon the name Jesus at the slightest opportunity – when they are scared, happy, excited, etc. But who is Jesus? Who is He to you? Do you know Him? What do you know about Jesus? What is He to you? What can you tell others about Him? Do you think He is "a lie" who is merely being used to deceive multitudes?

The Man Jesus seeks to answer these and many more questions about Jesus, helping readers understand who He is, and showing them all they need to know about Him. This book seeks to reveal who Jesus Christ really is; He is not a lie. I hope to be able to paint a very clear picture of who He is and what His mission on earth was. This book will also explain the basis of His teachings and the power He carries; letting you into the secret of how you can tap into His power. The aim of this book is to take you through the journey of discovering the truth about Jesus Christ for yourself.

Everyone needs to know Jesus personally, not just knowing about Him. This knowledge should automatically graduate into each one striking up and developing a personal relationship with Him. This book will help everyone who does not yet have a personal knowledge and relationship with Jesus to do so. *The Man Jesus* will show you how to find Jesus.

Knowing Jesus Christ comes along with a lot of benefits. This book will reveal some of those benefits. Hopefully, they should motivate you to seek to know Christ the more. You will also learn how to enjoy a relationship with Him. All who know Jesus and have accepted Him as their Lord and Saviour have a rich inheritance in Him. You will discover them in this book. It is hoped that those who are truly searching for the truth of who Jesus is would find it in this book. Jesus Christ is the Way, the Truth, and the Life. A discovery of this revelation will change and transform your life for good.

Chapter One

Introducing Jesus

Jesus Christ was introduced to me at age ten, and I accepted Him as my Lord and Saviour. I have never had any cause to regret being a believing Christian ever since. For me, every day with Jesus will always be sweeter than the day before.

My knowledge of Him as the Alpha and the Omega as written in Revelation 22:13 and that His life on earth was long prophesied before His birth deepens my faith in Him. It also assures me that I am on the right track and that those other prophecies that are yet to be fulfilled will surely come to pass.

I have discovered through the word of God and from personal experience that there is so much power in the name of Jesus and His blood. Now, I don't hesitate to engage His name and blood as the need arises. My experience with Jesus has been sweet. Therefore, let me introduce you to the Lord that has made a great difference in my life. My short time as a believing Christian has taught me that life without Christ is truly a life in crisis.

In The Beginning He Was

How well do you know Jesus? A person you understand is the person you can risk following. Knowing his origin and background makes it easier to trust him. Jesus Christ's story is well spelt out in the scriptures.

> *Jesus said to them, "Most assuredly, I say to you, before Abraham was, I AM."*

> John 8:58

In the beginning was the Word, and the Word was with God, and the Word was God. He was in the beginning with God. All things were made through Him, and without Him nothing was made that was made...

And the Word became flesh and dwelt among us, and we beheld His glory, the glory as of the only begotten of the Father, full of grace and truth.

John 1:1-3, 14

Then God said, "Let Us make man in Our image, according to Our likeness; let them have dominion over the fish of the sea, over the birds of the air, and over the cattle, over all the earth and over every creeping thing that creeps on the earth."

Genesis 1:26

Jesus Christ existed since the beginning of creation. He is not a man who only surfaced in the New Testament. He existed right from the time of God the Creator. He only became flesh and dwelt among men in the New Testament, during the time of the apostles.

All things were made through Jesus; there was nothing made without Him. That was why God said in Genesis 1:26, *"Let Us make man in Our image..."* Jesus confirmed His existence long before the New Testament when He said to the Pharisees, *"Before Abraham was, I Am."*

Christ is your maker and the creator of all you can see. He knows you better than you know yourself. Since He has existed from the beginning, He understands this world and its system more than any other person. That means He is the best consultant on all world operations, including spiritual matters also. He is the most reliable force to camp with, as He knows all the devices of the enemy and has counter attack strategies with which to defeat the devil anytime and anywhere.

Even demons confirmed Jesus' existence before the New Testament. On seeing Jesus, two demon-possessed men cried out to Him in Matthew 8:29, *"What have we to do with You, Jesus, You Son of God? Have You come here to torment us before the time?"*

Jesus has been from the beginning; the demons know it and the spiritual and wise persons know it too.

Jesus has no superior other than God the Father, because He existed from the beginning. This, therefore, makes Him a great authority to be reckoned with. There is no opposition that can match Him. Lucifer, the devil, was created by God (Ezekiel 28:12-15) through Jesus, and so cannot be compared with Him.

If Jesus is with you and for you, be assured of His continuous presence with you, as He has promised never to leave you nor forsake you (Hebrews 13:5). He again promised in Matthew 28:20 to be with you always, even to the end of the age. He can make such promises because He has been from the beginning and knows that He will continue to be till the end of the age.

Jesus has been with God from the beginning (John 1:1), and so is your best access to God. He Himself said in John 14:6 that no one can come to God except through Him. So if you have been trying to reach God, congratulations; Jesus is your access to the Father, you need not search any further. Christ is the eternal way to God the Father!

Prophecies Fulfilled

How many people do you know of whose lives were prophesied before they were born? Long before He was born, virtually everything about Jesus' life was prophesied! This means He is not a fake, and that He means business.

Jesus is the perfect proof of the fact that God, the architect of your life, already has a plan for your life. This plan will be developed as you grow, if you will obey His instructions and walk in His footsteps.

Let's consider some of the prophecies about Jesus, as well as their fulfillment.

- **Jesus was to be born of a woman.**

    After the fall of man, God quickly made a plan to restore man to his original state and fellowship with Him. In Genesis 3:15, God said He would put enmity between Satan and the woman, and between his seed and her Seed. The Seed of the woman shall bruise Satan's head, and Satan would bruise His heel. Jesus was born of a woman (Matthew 1:20-25). He finished or "bruised" Satan's head (Colossians 2:15), but Satan could only hurt Him a little (Matthew 27:46).

- **He would be a descendant of the patriarchs - Abraham, Isaac and Jacob** (Genesis 21:12; 22:18; Numbers 24:17). This was fulfilled in Luke 3:34 and Romans 9:5. Now, among other things, the blessings of Abraham as God promised him in Genesis 12:1-3, can now come to all who believe through Jesus Christ (Galatians 3:14).

- **He would come from the tribe of Judah** (Genesis 49:10). God, through Jacob, prophesied that the sceptre will not depart from Judah, nor a lawgiver from between his feet. This was again fulfilled in Luke 3:33 and confirmed in Hebrews 7:14. Jesus is the only King that lives forever, and He is from the tribe of Judah according to the flesh. Kings were to come from the tribe of Judah, so Christ had to come from that tribe, since He was the King of the Jews.

- **Jesus Christ would be the heir to the throne of David** (2 Samuel 7:12-13; Isaiah 9:6-7). God's promise to David, to establish his seed over his throne forever was fulfilled in Jesus in Luke 1:30-33 and Romans 1:3. No wonder when blind Bartimaeus called Him the "Son of David", it caught His attention, and He quickly responded to Bartimaeus' demands (Mark 10:46-52).

- **He would be born of a virgin** (Isaiah 7:14). Isaiah prophesied that a virgin would conceive and bear a son, whose name would be called Immanuel (fulfilled in Matthew 1:20-23). Jesus had to be born of a virgin and the Holy Spirit, so that He is born of God, and free of the Adamic nature that is characterized by sin.

- **He would be born in Bethlehem and stay in Egypt for a while** (Micah 5:2; Hosea 11:1). Jesus' place of birth was fulfilled in Luke 2:1-7. A decree had to go out that the entire world should be registered so that the Messiah would be born in the City of David, which is called

Bethlehem, just as was prophesied by prophet Micah. After Jesus' birth, again in fulfillment of Hosea's prophecy, Joseph fled to Egypt with the baby, for fear of Herod finding and killing Him (Matthew 2:13-15). That means that even some seeming minute details of your life, for example, where you were born, is orchestrated by God.

- **John the Baptist was to prepare the way for Christ** (Isaiah 40:3-5). A voice was to cry out in the wilderness, *"Prepare the way of the Lord..."* The voice turned out to be John the Baptist (Luke 3:3-6). Malachi 4:5-6 prophesied that Elijah would come before the great day of the Lord, before the Messiah would come. Jesus confirmed John as the Elijah that was to come in Matthew 11:13-14.

- **Speaking in parables.** Have you ever wondered why Jesus spoke and taught a lot in parables? It was prophesied that He would do so (Psalm 78:2-4), and was again fulfilled (Matthew 13:34-35).

- **Declaration of His mission on the earth** (Isaiah 61:1-2). Isaiah prophesied that Jesus would be anointed by God to preach good tidings to the poor, heal the brokenhearted, proclaim liberty to the captives, and the opening of the prison to those who are bound. He was also to proclaim the acceptable year of the Lord, and the day of vengeance of our God. Lastly, Jesus came to comfort all who mourn. Jesus read out this exact prophecy in Luke 4:18-19, and in verse 21 declared to the people that this scripture was fulfilled in their hearing.

- **Details of Christ's crucifixion, resurrection and ascension.** Jesus' betrayal, crucifixion, resurrection and ascension were very detailed that anybody who cares to consider them would agree that Jesus is real. The amazing thing is that these details were recorded in scriptures long before Jesus' birth; and were all fulfilled to the letter.

  Let's look at some of them. Though some of these prophecies were recorded in more than one book in both the Old and New Testaments, we will look at only one each.

o **Jesus' betrayal.** This was clearly prophesied in the Old Testament.

Even my own familiar friend in whom I trusted, Who ate my bread, Has lifted up his heel against me.

Psalm 41:9

Judas Iscariot fulfilled this prophecy in Matthew 26:23-25, 47-50.

o **The betrayal price money.** It was prophesied that Jesus would be betrayed for thirty pieces of silver, and that the money would eventually be used to buy a potter's field (Zechariah 11:12-13). We saw this fulfilled in Matthew 27:9-10.

o **False accusation.** It was prophesied in Psalm 35:11 that Jesus would be falsely accused; and it was fulfilled in Mark 14:57-58.

o **Spat upon and beaten.** A prophecy said Jesus would be beaten and spat upon (Isaiah 50:6). We saw this fulfilled in Matthew 26:67.

- Mocked and ridiculed. Psalm 22:7-8 said Jesus would be mocked and ridiculed, it was fulfilled in Luke 23:35-39.

- Crucified along with two robbers. Isaiah 53:12 told us this would happen, and it was fulfilled in Mark 15:27-28.

- Given vinegar for a drink. This was prophesied in Psalm 69:21 and fulfilled in John 19:28-30.

- Hands and feet pierced. Jesus' hands and feet were pierced as prophesied in Psalm 22:16, and fulfilled in John 20:25-27.

- Sides pierced. Zechariah 12:10 also prophesied that Jesus' sides would be pierced. We see this fulfilled in John 19:34.

- Garments divided and lots cast for His clothing. Psalm 22:18 told us this would happen; and it was fulfilled in Matthew 27:35-36.

- Unbroken bones. Psalm 34:20 prophesied that Jesus' bones would not be broken (unlike the usual practice, where they broke the bones of the person crucified to hasten their death). Jesus died on the cross, so there was no need to break His bones (John 19:33-36).

o **To be forsaken by God the Father.** Psalm 22:1 told us well in advance that Jesus would be forsaken by God. We saw this fulfilled in Matthew 27:46, where God forsook Jesus, because all He saw in Him was the sins of the world that He bore.

o **Prayed for His accusers.** The scriptures prophesied in Psalm 109:4 that Jesus would do this; and it was fulfilled in Luke 23:34.

o **Resurrection from the dead.** Psalm 16:10 prophesied that Jesus would rise from the grave. Jesus truly rose from the grave as recorded in all the books of the gospels. Peter gave us a detailed account of how it happened in Acts 2:22-32.

o **Ascension into heaven.** Jesus' ascension into heaven is the grand finale of the redemption plan. It was prophesied in Psalm 24:7-10 and fulfilled in Mark 16:19.

o **Enthronement at God's right hand.** Jesus' ascension into heaven so He can be enthroned was prophesied in Psalm 110:1, and fulfilled in Mark 16:19

The Jews did all they did to Jesus without realising that they were fulfilling scriptures, the word of God. These events all prove that Jesus Christ came from God; as everything that was done to Him was as God had said through His prophets. Interestingly, King David had a lot to say (by the Spirit) about the seed that would be over his throne forever.

Prophet Isaiah in Isaiah 53:1-12 gave a very vivid description of the suffering that the Messiah would endure. He stated that Jesus would be a sacrifice for man's sins, which He fulfilled (Romans 5:6-8). Isaiah also declared that God would be satisfied with Jesus' sacrifice and divide Him a portion with the great. No wonder God exalted Him and gave Him a name above every other name, that at the name of Jesus every knee should bow, of those in heaven, and of those on earth, and of those under the earth, and that every tongue should confess that Jesus Christ is Lord, to the glory of God the Father (Philippians 2:5-11)!

Jesus Christ came to earth on an assignment; which He accomplished and returned to heaven afterwards. If all the prophecies given concerning His birth, death, resurrection and ascension all came to pass, one can safely conclude that in like manner the prophecies about His coming back (Acts 1:9-11, Revelation 22:6-21) and the events that will follow (recorded in the book of Revelation) will all surely come to pass.

Jesus' Mission

God is a God of purpose, Who does nothing without a reason. Jesus was sent to the earth by God for a purpose, which He accomplished. An understanding of this purpose will help you appreciate the coming of Christ and His mission on earth.

> *The Spirit of the Lord is upon Me,*
> *because He has anointed Me to*

preach the gospel to the poor; He has sent Me to heal the brokenhearted, to proclaim liberty to the captives and recovery of sight to the blind, to set at liberty those who are oppressed; to proclaim the acceptable year of the Lord.

Luke 4:18-19

And she will bring forth a Son, and you shall call His name Jesus, for He will save His people from their sins.

Matthew 1:21

Now all things are of God, who has reconciled us to Himself through Jesus Christ, and has given us the ministry of reconciliation, that is, that God was in Christ reconciling the world to Himself, not imputing their trespasses to them, and has committed to us the word of reconciliation. 2 Corinthians 5:18-19

The thief does not come except to steal, and to kill, and to destroy. I have come that they may have life, and that they may have it more abundantly.

John 10:10

Jesus Christ came to save man, reconcile them back to God and give them life in abundance. The strategy for accomplishing this was to preach the gospel, heal the sick, set the captives free, grant sight to the blind, deliver the oppressed, and ultimately proclaim the acceptable year of the Lord. God fully anointed Jesus to accomplish this mission (Acts 10:38).

- **The Salvation of Souls**

When the angel of the Lord visited Joseph to assure him that it was okay to take Mary as his wife, he gave him the name of the baby and his purpose on earth: to save His people from their sins (Matthew 1:21).

Right from when man fell in the Garden of Eden, God made a plan to redeem man from his fall and restore him to his original position of dominion and fellowship. Man was created without sin. As a result, he was lord over God's creation and enjoyed daily fellowship with God. Sin came in when Adam and Eve disobeyed God and ate of the forbidden fruit (Genesis 3:1-11). That was the introduction of sin into the world, and every person born of natural man is a sinner (Romans 5:12, 19).

Jesus is God's wisdom and power to save man from his sins and restore him to his original state before the fall (1 Corinthians 1:24). In Genesis 3:15, God declared this plan of victory over the devil – the Seed of the woman was to defeat the devil. The enemy expected it, tried to abort it many times but failed, because he didn't know how God was going to execute His plan.

When the birth of Jesus was announced to King Herod by the wise men from the east, the enemy tried to kill Jesus through Herod. But he again failed; he succeeded only in killing innocent babies (Matthew 2:1-18). When Jesus' earthly ministry began, the devil also tried to kill Him on several occasions using the people (Luke 4:28-30), but failed, because it wasn't yet time for Jesus to die; His mission on earth had to be concluded first (Luke 22:53).

The wisdom of God for man's restoration was a great mystery: if the devil had known it, he would not have allowed the people to crucify Jesus (1 Corinthians 2:7-8). He thought Christ's death would be his victory, not knowing it was going to be his downfall (Colossians 2:13-15).

Jesus Christ, who knew no sin, became sin, that we might be saved and become the righteousness of God (2 Corinthians 5:21). Jesus took our place on the cross; bearing our sins upon Himself so we can stand before God blameless. Our sins were washed away by His shed blood, and now as many as have accepted Him as Saviour can stand before God as totally new people; old things are passed away, and behold all things have become new (2 Corinthians 5:17).

God is of purer eyes than to behold iniquity (Habakkuk 1:13). When Jesus bore the sins of humanity on the cross, God had no choice but to turn His back on Him. That was why Jesus cried out, "My God, My God, why have you forsaken Me?" (Matthew 27:46). For the first time, Jesus addressed God as God, instead of Father as He had always done. But He achieved His purpose, which was to save man from his sin. Now anyone who receives Jesus as Lord and Saviour automatically receives the gift that has been fully paid for: the forgiveness of sins and the salvation of soul.

- **Reconciliation Unto God**

Before the fall of man, man had great fellowship with God. On the day of Adam's disobedience, the Bible records that the Lord came in the cool of the day calling on Adam (Genesis 3:8). This suggests that an intimate relationship between God and man existed before the fall. This relationship, however, came to an end, and God had to drive the man and his wife out of the Garden of Eden, ending their fellowship.

Part of God's plan of salvation for man was to reconcile man back to Himself through Christ, forgiving and forgetting the sin that had put up the barrier between them. Jesus made peace between God and man through His shed blood on the cross (Colossians 1:20).

Every believing Christian now receives the spirit of adoption at new birth, by whom he cries out, "Abba, Father" (Romans 8:15). We can now relate with God as a father and son would, just as Adam did in the garden before the fall. Until you are born again, God is merely your maker or creator. But He becomes your Father when you received His Son, Jesus Christ, as your Saviour.

Jesus through His death has reconciled you to God, to present you holy, blameless and above reproach, in His sight. You can now come boldly unto the throne of grace to obtain mercy and find grace to help in time of need (Hebrews 4:16).

- **Abundant Life**

The enemy's mission on earth is to steal, kill and destroy; but Jesus Christ came to give man abundant life (John 10:10). Everyone who has left houses, brothers, sisters, father, mother, wife, children or lands for Christ's sake shall surely receive them many times more in this present time, and in the age to come eternal life (Matthew 19:29). This is abundant life.

Galatians 3:13-14 clearly states that Christ hung on the cross in order to deliver the blessings of Abraham to us as God had promised in Genesis 12:1-3: *"In you shall all families be blessed."* Abraham became a great nation and a blessing; those who blessed him were blessed by God, whereas those who cursed him were cursed by God. Abraham enjoyed abundant life, and Christ hung on the cross that we may be partakers of the Abrahamic order of blessings.

Abundant life is life without sickness or disease, filled with wealth and riches, coupled with tremendous spiritual growth (3 John 2). It is also a life full of power, riches, wisdom, strength, honour, glory and blessings (Revelation 5:12). Abundant life includes longevity (Psalm 91:16). Like Paul, you too can decide when you want to return to your Father in heaven (Philippians 1:21-26).

In conclusion, Jesus Christ's mission on earth was to obey God (Hebrews 10:5-7) and to restore man to his original spiritual state, so he could enjoy unlimited access to God and to all that He has to offer (Romans 8:17).

God's Mystic Secret Unveiled

Does God have secrets? Yes, He does. The good news, however, is that they are now revealed to His children by His Holy Spirit. What's more, knowing God's secret is vital to living a life of absolute victory.

> *...And that they may become progressively more intimately acquainted with and may know more definitely and accurately and*

thoroughly that mystic secret of God,
[which is] Christ (the Anointed One).

Colossians 2:2 (AMP)

But we speak the wisdom of God in a
mystery, the hidden wisdom which
God ordained before the ages for our
glory, which none of the rulers of
this age knew; for had they known,
they would not have crucified the
Lord of glory.

1 Corinthians 2:7, 8

And I will put enmity between you
and the woman, and between your
offspring and her Offspring; He will
bruise and tread your head
underfoot, and you will lie in wait
and bruise His heel.

Genesis 3:15 (AMP)

Praise God, the mystic secret of God has been revealed! God's mystery came into existence at the fall of man. When the enemy did his worst by making man fall through his deceit, God created this mystery with which He was to overthrow the enemy and recover all for Himself and for man. Though He said it out loudly then, the enemy did not understand it; if he had, he would not have crucified the Lord of Glory, Jesus (1 Corinthians 2:8).

That day in the Garden of Eden, God said He would put enmity between the devil and the woman, and between his offspring and her Offspring. According to God, the woman's Offspring would bruise and tread the devil's head underfoot, and the devil will lie in wait and bruise His heel. This was fulfilled in Jesus.

> *But when the proper time had fully come, God sent His Son, born of a woman, born subject to [the regulations of] the Law,*
> *To purchase the freedom of (to ransom, to redeem, to atone for) those who were subject to the Law, that we might be adopted and have*

sonship conferred upon us [and be
recognized as God's sons].

Galatians 4:4-5 (AMP)

What exactly is this mystic secret of God? It is Jesus Christ, the anointed one! Some of the great men in the Old Testament, like Moses, David and Isaiah (Deuteronomy 18:15; Acts 2:23-36; Isaiah 9:6-7) had an idea of this mystery, but the full picture was not revealed until Christ was born, crucified, resurrected and seated at the right hand of God. Victory at last!

• **Why Christ?**

Why was Jesus Christ God's mystic secret? If God was to achieve perfection as it was before the fall of man, he needed Jesus, Who is God and without sin, but born of a woman, because the world was supposed to be under man's control till an appointed time (1 Corinthians 15:25). Adam had sold out to the enemy, and because his lease on earth had not run out, God had to get another man

(Jesus Christ) to overthrow the enemy and recover all, both man and the earth.

The Significance of Jesus' Names

Names are very significant to the life of any individual. It describes the destiny, purpose and character of the person. It actually dictates his steps or decisions. Therefore, a good name will speak well of an individual, whereas a bad name will speak ill of him/her. In this section, we will consider the many names of Jesus Christ, and how they defined His nature, mission and destiny.

> *For unto us a Child is born, unto us a Son is given; and the government will be upon His shoulder. And His name will be called Wonderful, Counselor, Mighty God, Everlasting Father, Prince of Peace.*
>
> Isaiah 9:6

> *And she will bring forth a Son, and you shall call His name JESUS, for*

He will save His people from their sins.

God uses names to pass across messages to men. When God names your unborn baby, He is directly telling you what to expect of the baby; He is simply prophesying into the life of the child. That is why it is good to receive your children's names from God. If you name your child yourself, know that the baby's life and destiny will be influenced by the meaning of its given name.

A name brings out the best or the worst of a person. It can also accelerate or hinder his success in life, bring joy and peace to his life, or sorrow and misery. The Bible makes this very clear in 1 Samuel 25:25: *"Please, let not my lord regard this scoundrel Nabal. For as his name is, so is he: Nabal is his name, and folly is with him!"* A name will surely affect the bearer positively or negatively; therefore, it is important that we give our children godly names. The names we give them should help them succeed in life.

God changed Abraham's name from Abram to Abraham to describe what he would later become – a father of many nations (Genesis 17:5-6). Just as his name, Abraham truly became the father of nations. He is the father of both the physical nation of Israel and all spiritual Israelites, that is, everyone redeemed by the blood of Jesus Christ.

Before God changed his name to Israel, Jacob was living out his name (a sup-planter) to the full. He supplanted Esau twice: when he took away his birth right and blessing by deception (Genesis 27:36). But he got a change of name in Genesis 32:24-28, after he wrestled with an angel and prevailed. Jacob asked the angel to bless him, and the blessing he got was a change of name! His new name reflected his new destiny. Names truly speak a lot about an individual.

Jesus was equally not exempted from the influence of names. His names said a lot about His life and destiny. Let's consider a few of them:

- **Jesus** – Saviour (Matthew 1:21)
- **Immanuel** – God with us (Matthew 1:23)

- **Jehovah** – The Lord (Isaiah 40:3)
- **The Redeemer** (Isaiah 59:20)
- **The Word** – (John 1:1)
- **The Hope of His people** – (Joel 3:16)
- **Son of man** – (Mark 10:33)
- **Son of David** – (Matthew 1:1)
- **Seed of the woman** (Genesis 3:15)
- **Seed of Abraham** (Galatians 3:16)
- **Lamb of God** (John 1:29)
- **The Lamb that was slain** (Revelation 5:12)
- **The Good Shepherd** (John 10:11)
- **Bread of life** (John 6:35)
- **The light of the world** (John 8:12)
- **The Wisdom of God** (1 Corinthians 1:24)
- **The Power of God** (1 Corinthians 1:24)
- **The Rock** (1 Corinthians 10:4)
- **The Mediator** (1 Timothy 2:5)
- **The Intercessor** (Hebrews 7:25)
- **The Advocate** (1 John 2:1)
- **The Last Adam** (1 Corinthians 15:45)
- **The Resurrection** (John 11:25)
- **A Quickening Spirit** (1 Corinthians 15:45)

+ **The Deliverer** (Romans 11:26)

+ **The Lion of the Tribe of Judah** (Revelation 5:5)

+ **Lord of lords** (Revelation 17:14)

+ **King of kings** (Revelation 17:14)

+ **Lord of all** (Acts 10:36)

+ **Lord over all** (Romans 10:12)

+ **The Prince of Peace** (Isaiah 9:6)

+ **The Beginning and the Ending** (Revelation 1:8)

+ **The Alpha and the Omega** (Revelation 1:8)

+ **The First and the Last** (Revelation 1:17)

+ **My Portion** (Jeremiah 10:16)

+ **My Helper** (Hebrews 13:6)

+ **My Physician** (Jeremiah 8:22)

+ **My Healer** (Luke 9:11)

+ **My Restorer** (Psalm 23:3)

+ **My All in All** (Colossians 3:11)

Jesus Christ the Saviour came to save the world, so that as many as would receive Him would be saved. Being the Word, Jesus makes it clear that the scriptures are centred on Him.

Jesus needed to be the Son of man in order to save man from his sins. God needed a man like Adam to restore man back to fellowship, glory and dominion. Adam (man) had been put in charge of the world (as its ruler) for a season, and his time was not yet over before Satan stole it from him. Jesus needed to be the Son of man to accomplish His purpose of recovering man and the earth. That was also the only way of fulfilling God's word to the serpent, that the Seed of the woman would bruise his head (Genesis 3:15).

Jesus Christ also needed to be the Seed of Abraham, so we could partake of the blessings of Abraham (Galatians 3:13-14). He had to be the Son of David to fulfil God's promise to King David that his seed would reign on his throne forever.

Since lambs were slain for the atonement of the people's sins under the Old Covenant, Christ had to be the Lamb that was slain once and for all for the atonement of the sins of the whole world in the New Covenant. As the Good Shepherd, He had to lay down His life for His sheep.

Christ is the Bread of life whom when eaten, gives life in abundance. As the Light of the world, He is the perfect guide to follow in order not to stumble in this world, no matter the challenge. Jesus is full of wonders and will always give the right counsel.

Jesus is the wisdom and the power of God by which God defeated the enemy, making a public show of him, triumphing over him. He is the Rock, so can be sure of His support always. He is our advocate, and is seated at God's right hand in heaven interceding continually on our behalf. He is The Lord of lords and King of kings, and so is Lord of all and over all. Everyone and all powers are subject to Jesus.

Do you desire peace? Jesus, the Prince of peace, is the best authority to consult on that matter. As the Beginning and the Ending, the First and the Last, be rest assured that nothing is hid from Him, neither is there anything new or strange to Him. If you will receive Him as your portion, then all that belongs to Him becomes yours automatically. As your Helper, you will enjoy unending helps; and as your Physician or Healer, you will enjoy total health and vitality. Indeed, Jesus Christ is all in all; so you are fully covered on every side.

Jesus truly is the Way, the Truth and the Life (John 14:6). No one can come to the Father except through Him. You need not fear ever again if you receive Him as Lord and Saviour, because His name is a strong tower which the righteous runs into and are safe (Proverbs 18:10).

Power in the Name Jesus

Not only does Jesus' name reflect His mission and destiny, it is also full of power. His name has power to save from sin, as salvation comes only through calling upon the name of Jesus (Romans 10:13; Acts 4:12). Also, answer to prayers is only guaranteed if made in the name of Jesus (John 14:14; 15:16; 16:23). Healing comes through putting your faith in His name as well.

And His name, through faith in his name, has made this man strong, whom ye see and know. Yes, the faith which comes through Him has given him this perfect soundness in the presence of you all.

Acts 3:16

The name of Jesus is very powerful. Unfortunately many are ignorant of this power, and so are being robbed of God's blessings and fulfilment in life. The enemy will do anything to keep a man in this ignorant state so he can continue to oppress him. The truth is that the power in the name of Jesus brings deliverance from all oppressions of the devil, and delivers dominion to mankind.

God, understanding the power of a name, carefully chose Jesus' name to reflect His mission on earth and after resurrection. The name Jesus means Saviour.

Nor is there salvation in any other, for there is no other name under

heaven given among men by which
we must be saved.

Acts 4:12

Salvation means deliverance from sin and its consequences. It also means preservation or deliverance from harm, ruin or loss. In other words, there can be no deliverance from sin and its consequences, nor preservation or deliverance from harm, ruin or loss, except through the name of Jesus.

To fully enjoy the benefits in the name of Jesus, you must first understand the power it carries. What can the name of Jesus do for you?

- **It Gives Identity**

  ...And the disciples were first called Christians in Antioch.

Acts 11:26

Your belief in Jesus and His name is what gives you your identity as a Christian. What's more? You are also expected to live like Him!

- **Name Above All Other Names**

  Therefore God also has highly exalted Him and given Him the name which is above every name, that at the name of Jesus every knee should bow, of those in heaven, and of those on earth, and of those under the earth, and that every tongue should confess that Jesus Christ is Lord, to the glory of God the Father.

  Philippians 2:9-11

The name Jesus is above the name of any sickness, disease or situation. Whatever has a name is below the name of Jesus and must give way to it when invoked, no matter where it may be coming from, whether from heaven, earth or hell.

- **Receiving From God**

  "And in that day you will ask Me nothing. Most assuredly, I say to you, whatever you ask the Father in My name He will give you. Until now you have asked nothing in My name.

Ask, and you will receive, that your joy may be full.

God's grand design for receiving from Him is through Jesus and His name. After His death and resurrection, no man can relate with God except through Jesus. He is the gateway to God and His blessings. Jesus is man's only access to God and all His blessings, including healing.

- **Name As Powerful As His Person**

Jesus' name is as powerful as His person. Everything He is can be found in His name. No wonder Jesus said to His disciples:

And these signs will follow those who believe: In My name they will cast out demons; they will speak with new tongues; they will take up serpents; and if they drink anything deadly, it will by no means hurt them; they will lay hands on the sick, and they will recover."

Mark 16:17-18

Whatever Jesus can do in person, the power in His name will deliver the same when you use it by faith. Whatever God says you can do, you can do in the name of Jesus. You can say, "Let there be…in Jesus' name," and it will be as you have spoken. Our God-given authority can only be exercised in the name of Jesus.

- **Always Working**

Jesus' name is ever at work, no matter what time of the day you use it. In the same way Jesus is alive and always with the believer, His name will deliver your desired results whenever you use it or call upon it.

> *I am He who lives, and was dead, and behold, I am alive forevermore. Amen. And I have the keys of Hades and of Death.*
>
> Revelations 1:18
>
> *Teaching them to observe all things that I have commanded you; and lo, I am with you always, even to the end of the age." Amen*   Matthew 28:20

43

- **Enemies Bow To The Name**

The enemy knows and understands the power of names, especially the power in the name of Jesus. He trembles at the mention of the name of Jesus.

> *And behold, they shrieked and screamed, What have You to do with us, Jesus, Son of God? Have You come to torment us before the appointed time?*
>
> Matthew 8:29 (AMP)

Just as devils trembled at the presence of Jesus, they also tremble at the mention of His name.

> *And she did this for many days. Then Paul, being sorely annoyed and worn out, turned and said to the spirit within her, I charge you in the name of Jesus Christ to come out of her! And it came out that very moment.*
>
> Acts 16:18 (AMP)

You can command healing or deliverance over your life or that of your loved ones in the name of

Jesus, and the spirit of infirmity will have no choice but to leave immediately.

- **The Name Is A Strong Refuge**

  The name of the Lord is a strong tower; the righteous run to it and are safe.

Proverbs 18:10

The power in the name of Jesus provides protection and covering for those that believe in it. When you call upon His name in times of danger, Jesus quickly shields you from any imminent evil. Instant results and deliverance are also guaranteed when you call upon the name.

And Peter said to him, "Aeneas, Jesus the Christ heals you. Arise and make your bed." Then he arose immediately.

Acts 9:34

Help and answers are dispatched immediately when you call on the name of Jesus. In most cases you receive instant help, while in some cases help comes as you learn to walk in obedience to God's word.

Note, however, that the name of Jesus must be invoked in faith for it to deliver the desired result. Calling upon the name without faith in your heart is an exercise in futility (Acts 3:16).

Faith in the name of Jesus is the secret of its power. Unbelief or a careless use of the name will not work. Always mention it in faith and with an understanding of the power that lies therein. Don't call His name in vain; for this is unacceptable with God.

Also note that only born again children of God are permitted to use the name of Jesus.

> *Then some of the itinerant Jewish exorcists took it upon themselves to call the name of the Lord Jesus over those who had evil spirits, saying, "We exorcise you by the Jesus whom Paul preaches." Also there were seven sons of Sceva, a Jewish chief priest, who did so.*

And the evil spirit answered and said, "Jesus I know, and Paul I know; but who are you?"

Then the man in whom the evil spirit was leaped on them, overpowered them, and prevailed against them, so that they fled out of that house naked and wounded. This became known both to all Jews and Greeks dwelling in Ephesus; and fear fell on them all, and the name of the Lord Jesus was magnified.

Acts 19:13-17

It is very dangerous to use the name of Jesus if you have not first identified with Him. You have to first give your life to Jesus before you can enjoy the power in His name. There is healing and deliverance in the name of Jesus; so go ahead and use it over that illness or situation in your life right now.

The Powerful Blood of Jesus

Not only is Jesus' name full of power, His blood is as well. Every covenant is sealed or ratified with blood. The New Testament or covenant was sealed with the blood of Jesus; that is why the Christian faith is anchored on the shed blood of Jesus Christ. An understanding of its power and benefits will help you put your faith in it, so you can enjoy all that it has to offer.

> *And they overcame him by the blood of the Lamb and by the word of their testimony, and they did not love their lives to the death.*
>
> Revelation 12:11

> *But we speak the wisdom of God in a mystery, the hidden wisdom which God ordained before the ages for our glory, which none of the rulers of this age knew; for had they known, they would not have crucified the Lord of glory.*
>
> 1 Corinthians 2:7-8

Then Jesus said to them, "Most assuredly, I say to you, unless you eat the flesh of the Son of Man and drink His blood, you have no life in you.

Whoever eats My flesh and drinks My blood has eternal life, and I will raise him up at the last day.

For My flesh is food indeed, and My blood is drink indeed. He who eats My flesh and drinks My blood abides in Me, and I in him. As the living Father sent Me, and I live because of the Father, so he who feeds on Me will live because of Me.

John 6:53-57

In the Old Testament, almost all things were purified with animal blood. There was also no remission without the shedding of blood (Hebrews 9:22). The blood was used for the cleansing, sanctification and consecration of both things and people. The blood was very important for their continual existence. Since the blood of bulls and goats had no capacity to permanently take away sins, it had to be shed repeatedly (Hebrews 10:1-4).

But the blood of Jesus Christ is different; it is so powerful that it was shed once and for all for the remission of all of man's sins!

> *Therefore, when He came into the world, He said: "Sacrifice and offering You did not desire, but a body You have prepared for Me. In burnt offerings and sacrifices for sin You had no pleasure. Then I said, 'Behold, I have come— in the volume of the book it is written of Me—to do Your will, O God.'"...*
>
> *For by one offering He has perfected forever those who are being sanctified.*
>
> Hebrews 10:5-14

By the shed blood of Jesus, sin and its consciousness is now totally removed from those who have put their faith in it and accepted to be cleansed by it!

The great power in the blood of Jesus is the only reason God allowed His Son's blood to be shed. In addition to our sins being washed away by Christ's blood, our conscience is also purged from dead works by the blood (Hebrews 9:14). If only the rulers of this age knew the power that is in the blood of Jesus, they would not have crucified Him! Jesus' blood grants every believer direct access to the Holiest of all. Before Jesus' death and His shed blood, only the high priest could go into the Holiest of all, and that only once a year. He must also go in with the blood of animal, which he offers for his sins and that of the people (Hebrews 9:6-8). But now, through the shed blood of Jesus Christ, every redeemed child of God can enter freely into the Holiest of all – God's presence (Hebrews 10:19). We all can now boldly come into the throne of grace in prayer and obtain mercy and grace by Christ's blood. You only need to accept the sacrifice of Jesus on the cross for your sins in order to qualify to enter.

Christ through His blood, reconciled man back to God, so that man can once again fellowship with God without the sin barrier. If you have accepted Jesus as the Lord of your life, you are now justified by His blood. You are now a new creation; old things are passed away, behold all things have become new (2 Corinthians 5:17-19).

The blood of Jesus also grants us victory. Believers can overcome the devil and his temptations by the blood of the Lamb, Jesus Christ (Revelations 12:11). That is why the Bible says that if the rulers (the enemy and his agents) had known what was coming to them by the death of Jesus they wouldn't have crucified the Lord of glory (1 Corinthians 2:7-8). Jesus died as a man (flesh and blood), so that through His death He might destroy him who had the power of death, that is the devil, and release those who through the fear of death were all their lifetime subject to bondage (Hebrews 2:14-15).

Many are held captive by the fear of death, which is the enemy's most effective weapon against man. But when they know the power in the blood of Jesus and apply it, they would be set free and then be able to take the right steps that would enable them walk away from the challenges.

When Jesus died as a man, He qualified to take back from the devil the authority and power he had stolen from Adam. Jesus went to hell and took the keys of hell and of death from the enemy, and freed the saints who were in bondage of death (Revelations 1:17-18; Matthew 27:52-53). From then on, as many as receive Jesus Christ are freed from the bondage of death. The power in the blood of Jesus Christ weakens the enemy, causing him to let go of your goods and blessings.

The blood of Jesus also gives us eternal life - the ultimate goal and desire of every believer (John 3:16). When you receive the sacrifice of Jesus on the cross, you also receive everlasting life with God. There's life after death, and the blood of Jesus gives you access to that life with God and an escape from life with the devil. But this is not the eternal life God is talking about. Jesus tells us in John 17:3 what eternal life really is.

> *And this is eternal life, that they may know You, the only true God, and Jesus Christ whom You have sent.*

Eternal life is knowing God and Jesus Christ whom God has sent. It is having a close, intimate, personal relationship with God and Jesus Christ. Everlasting life is not what you wait till you get to heaven to get or enjoy; it is what you get and start enjoying as soon as you believe in Jesus (John 3:36). God's greatest desire is that we all have a personal relationship with Him.

Adam had eternal life but lost it when He disobeyed God in the Garden of Eden. God had told them not to eat or touch the fruit of the tree which was in the midst of the garden (the tree of the knowledge of good and evil), lest they die (Genesis 2:16-17). When they both ate from the tree, they didn't die a physical death, but a spiritual one. They lost the intimate relationship they had enjoyed with God. God used to come down and commune with them. But they lost this sweet fellowship to sin and disobedience.

This fellowship was what God restored back to man through the shed blood of Jesus: that whosoever believes in Jesus would not perish, but have everlasting life. Oh, the power in Jesus blood!

Chapter 2

The Life and Examples of Jesus

The former account I made, O Theophilus, of all that Jesus began both to do and teach,

Acts 1:1

Jesus lived by examples when He was here on earth. He did nothing except what He saw His Father do, and spoke only as commanded by God (John 5:19; 8:28). Jesus taught only what He did, and has called us to live like Him. No wonder His disciples were called Christians in Antioch; for the people took notice of them that they behaved like Christ (Acts 11:26). They also did what they saw their master do, just as He did what He saw His Father do.

What were some outstanding things Jesus did during His earthly ministry? What examples did He leave for us to follow?

A Man of Prayers

Now in the morning, having risen a long while before daylight, He went out and departed to a solitary place; and there He prayed.

Mark 1:35

One notable thing Jesus did was that He prayed often (Luke 5:16). "Why would He pray when He is God?" you may wonder. People pray because they need a higher power to act on their behalf or help them solve one or more problems. Since Jesus is God, what was He doing praying?

Jesus prayed at every opportunity He had, and for various reasons. Prayer is the means through which we communicate with God. So Jesus prayed when He needed just to be in communion with His Father, when He needed to know what to do or wisdom from the Father, and even when He needed to overcome temptation.

Jesus Christ was born of a woman and so had the flesh that is limited. He needed to be in constant communion with God the Father, so they can

58

remain in fellowship. He also needed God to guide Him on earth just like we humans do. Remember that everything He did was as directed by God (John 12:49-50). He got all His instructions and directions from God through prayers.

For instance, before commencing His full-time ministry, He did a forty days prayer and fasting, after which He returned into Galilee in the power of the Holy Spirit, and His fame spread abroad through all the regions (Luke 4:1-15). He needed the anointing for ministry from God, and got it through prayers. At another time, Christ prayed all night before choosing His twelve disciples (Luke 6:12-16). Apparently, God gave Him the names of those He chose during the night prayers, including Judas Iscariot who betrayed Him.

Before He was betrayed and His journey to the cross, He prayed harder than ever before for grace to bear what lay ahead of Him. He prayed so much so that His sweat was like great drops of blood, and the angel of God came and strengthened Him (Luke 22:41-44). It was from here that He received the grace to face the betrayal, shame, persecution, crucifixion and death without giving up. The greatest challenge before Him was how to face the trauma of being rejected by the Father when He carried all our sins (Matthew 27:46). Praise God He received strength and encouragement to overcome through prayers!

Jesus Christ fellowshipped with His Father through prayers. He drank of the love of the Father in prayers and then came out to face the hostility of men towards Him without being disturbed by it. Prayer, I believe, was His resting place from the day's hard work in the midst of sinful and spiritually blind men.

In prayers He could relate with God as a son relates with a father that loves him. No wonder prayer time was a great time for Him. He once prayed to God at the tomb of Lazarus, and part of what He said was, *"I thank You that You have heard Me. I know You always hear Me, but because of the people who are standing by I said this, that they may believe that You sent Me"* (John

11:41-42). This tells us how much Jesus enjoyed praying.

His disciples saw Him withdraw ever so often to pray and talk with His Father. They must have loved what they saw Him do, prompting them to ask Him, *"Lord, teach us to pray"* (Luke 11:1). Is it any wonder then that they too desired nothing more than to pray (Acts 6:4)? We too need to pray without ceasing if we desire fellowship with God.

Being in communion and fellowship with the Father empowered Jesus to live a victorious life. He was always refreshed and received wisdom, guidance and instructions from His Father when He prayed; so wisdom demands that He prayed continually. He left us an example to follow. If we too desire to live victorious lives we must do as He did (1 John 2:6).

Jesus prayed all-night long before selecting His twelve disciples. Following His example, the disciples also had to pray before selecting Judas' replacement (Acts 1:14-26). Prayer was an important part of Christ's earthly ministry, and He taught His disciples to follow in His footsteps. No wonder Paul admonished us to pray without ceasing (1 Thessalonians 5:17).

How Long Did Jesus Pray?

We are not told the specific number of minutes, hours or days that Jesus prayed. He prayed for as long as the issue on ground demanded. However, I believe most of His quiet times with God were not less than one hour, because He wondered why His disciples could not watch (pray) with Him for just one hour (Matthew 26:40).

Sometimes, Jesus prayed for only few minutes, like when He prayed before the tomb of Lazarus. Other times He prayed for hours, like after He had dismissed the five thousand men, besides women and children, that He fed with fives loaves and two fishes. He went and prayed from evening time till the fourth watch of the night before joining His disciples in the boat (Matthew 14:23-25). Sometimes, He prayed all night long, like His prayer before choosing His twelve disciples. At another time, He spent forty days fasting and praying before He started His ministry on earth.

The more you spend time in God's presence, the more your flesh is subdued and your spirit gains dominion and you become more spiritually alert to hear clearly from God. This guarantees your victory in the physical over all devices of the enemy. You get the details of the day ahead in prayer, causing you to go through the day victoriously as Christ would. So, don't rush through your quiet time.

Note that sometimes you may spend a long time praying to receive just one word from God. But that one word will save you years of toiling and frustration. Moses spent forty days and nights fasting before the Lord, in order to receive the Ten Commandments from God, by which the Israelites were governed for years before the new covenant with Christ (Exodus 34:28-29). Jesus spent the whole night in prayers before choosing His disciples, who later facilitated the spread of the gospel to the entire world. Therefore, the bigger the issue, the more time you should spend praying. Prayer was a big deal with Jesus. His success on earth hinged on the time He spent in God's presence praying. He left us an example to follow; and wisdom demands that you do as He did, if you want to enjoy fellowship with God as well as success in life.

Success Secret

Have you ever wondered how Jesus succeeded on earth to the point that His words and acts are still being celebrated today, and His followers are increasing by the hour? Jesus came on a mission which He finished within a short but good record time. What could have been His success secrets?

> *And He who sent Me is with Me. The Father has not left Me alone, for I always do those things that please Him.*

> John 8:29

How God anointed Jesus of Nazareth with the Holy Spirit and with power, who went about doing good and healing all who were oppressed by the devil, for God was with Him.

Acts 10:38

And being found in appearance as a man, He humbled Himself and became obedient to the point of death, even the death of the cross. Therefore God also has highly exalted Him and given Him the name which is above every name,

Philippians 2:8-9

Jesus' ministry on earth was only for three and half years, yet was so impactful and successful. Within this period He laid an unshakeable foundation that His disciples are still building upon today and will continue to build on till He returns. His success secrets are able to reproduce the same success story in your life if you care to act upon them.

- **Obedience**

Jesus was always obedient to His Father's instructions. He came to the earth in the first place in obedience to His Father. God needed someone to redeem man from sin, and so sent Christ to die for the sins of the world (Galatians 4:4-5). Throughout His stay on earth, Jesus lived a life of total obedience unto God, which enabled Him to carry God's presence all the time (John 8:29).

According to John 3:2, no man can do the miracles that Jesus did except God is with him. In other words, Christ's obedience to God led to the miracles that occurred through Him. Furthermore, obedience led to His name being exalted above every other name (Philippians 2:9).

- **Wisdom**

Though Jesus was the wisdom of God (1 Corinthians 1:24), He still needed to be filled with wisdom to be able to succeed in His earthly assignment (Luke 2:40). On many occasions wisdom was what helped Him to overcome the evil plots of the Pharisees. His teachings were also filled with wisdom applications.

When they brought the woman caught in adultery to Him in John 8:3-11, Jesus through wisdom gave the Pharisees no room to accuse Him, while at the same time rescuing the woman from being stoned to death.

His teachings and manner of teaching were so full of wisdom, that the people wondered how He got such wisdom, being only a "carpenter's son" (Matthew 13:54-55). His illustrations and ability to relate His teachings to everyday life made it easy for the people to understand and believe in Him.

- **Anointing**

The anointing was one major secret of Jesus' success here on earth.

> *How God anointed Jesus of Nazareth with the Holy Spirit and with power, who went about doing good and healing all who were oppressed by the devil, for God was with Him.*
>
> Acts 10:38

The anointing of God came upon Jesus at the onset of His ministry, and it enabled Him to go about doing good and healing all who were oppressed of the devil. Jesus returned in the power of the Holy Spirit (anointing) after His forty days of praying and fasting and temptation by the devil (Luke 4:14).

Jesus knew the importance of the anointing to His success, hence He instructed His disciples not to leave Jerusalem until they had been endued with the same power of the Holy Spirit (Acts 1:4, 8). The anointing was to enable them also fulfill their assignment as He had. The power of the anointing manifested in the life of Peter immediately after the baptism of the Holy Spirit, so much so that the same man who could not face a young girl before the death of Jesus was bold after being anointed to speak to multitudes, at the end of which three thousand men were added to the kingdom of God in one day (John 18:17; Acts 2:14-42)!

- **Humility**

Jesus' humility was legendary. It enabled Him to finish His earthly assignment in spite of the words and actions of the Pharisees and Jewish leaders against Him. Jesus endured the disrespect and insults of the same men He created so that He could carry out and finish His mission on the earth. Though He was God, being in the form of a man, He humbled Himself and became obedient to the point of death, even the death on the cross (Philippians 2:8).

Humility is a quality that attracts God to a man. God detests the proud (Proverbs 16:5), whereas He will guide the humble in justice and teach him His ways (Psalm 25:9). Jesus' humility caused Him to receive continual guidance from the Father, which helped Him succeed in His mission.

- **Self-awareness**

Christ knew who He was and believed in Himself and in His mission on earth. He didn't need any man's opinion of who He was, but God's approval. Self-awareness enabled Him to remain focused on

His assignment in spite of the numerous distractions. It also helped him to respond positively to people even when they were against Him. On the cross He asked God to forgive His crucifiers, because they knew not what they were doing (Luke 23:34).

Jesus was so aware of who He was that the soldiers sent to arrest Him returned to the Pharisees without Him (John 7:45-46). In John 4:1-42, we see the power of self-awareness at work in His life. The Samaritan woman who met Him at the well got saved along with virtually her whole city, simply because Jesus knew who He was. When His disciples urged Him to eat physical food, He said to them, *"My food is to do the will of Him who sent Me, and to finish His work"* (John 4:34).

- **Vision**

Jesus was a man of vision. Hebrews 12:2 tells us that Christ, for the joy that was set before Him, endured the cross, despising the shame, and is now seated at the right hand of the throne of God. This joy was His vision. The joy of being exalted at the right of God amongst the redeemed kept Him going even in the midst of heavy persecution.

Jesus envisioned God's kingdom being filled with the redeemed of the Lord and God the Father sitting with the multitudes that have been reconciled back to Him. This vision was so strong in Him that He told His disciples that He was going back to heaven to prepare a place for them (John 14:2-3).

Christ's desire was to please His Father, and one major way to do that was to restore man to his original state of fellowship and dominion before the fall. Jesus knowing how much God loved man and wanted man delivered from destruction, came and endured the cross to deliver His Father's greatest heart's desire. He had the vision to see the world saved from their sins and restored back to their original fellowship with God. That was His driving force and a secret of His success.

- **The Word Of God**

The Bible describes the word of God as a lamp unto our feet and a light unto our path (Psalm

119:105). Anyone who wants to succeed in life needs to have the word of God as his guide. Jesus Christ being the Word Himself (John 1:1-3, 14) was very conversant with the scriptures and used it as the need arose.

He used the word to defeat the devil when he tempted Him in the wilderness (Luke 4:1-13). And when He was given the book of Isaiah to read, He knew the very place that talked about Him and His assignment on earth. He read the verses to the people in the synagogue, introducing Himself and His mission to them (Luke 4:16-21).

Whenever the Jews accused Jesus of blasphemy, He would use the word of God to prove that He hadn't blasphemed, but only agreed with the word of God (John 10:33-36). Christ was born of the word and lived by the word.

- **Prayer**

Prayer is the power house of every believer, and Jesus never toyed with this powerful success tool. Like we said earlier, He engaged in forty days of fasting and prayer before commencing His earthly ministry, after which He returned to town in the power of the Holy Spirit (Luke 4:1-2, 14-15).

Jesus knew that prayer was vital to His success, so He prayed always – before choosing His twelve disciples, before His betrayal and crucifixion, early in the morning, after ministering to the people, when He needed to know what to do. Prayer was His source of spiritual reinforcement and the channel through which He received wisdom, instructions, guidance and directions from God. If Christ who is God needed to pray without ceasing, then we surely need to pray even more if success in life is our goal.

- **Delegation**

  After these things the Lord appointed seventy others also, and sent them two by two before His face into every city and place where He Himself was about to go. Then He said to them, "The harvest truly is great, but the laborers are few; therefore pray the

Lord of the harvest to send out laborers into His harvest.

Luke 10:1-2

And when He had called His twelve disciples to Him, He gave them power over unclean spirits, to cast them out, and to heal all kinds of sickness and all kinds of disease...

These twelve Jesus sent out and commanded them, saying: "Do not go into the way of the Gentiles, and do not enter a city of the Samaritans. But go rather to the lost sheep of the house of Israel. And as you go, preach, saying, 'The kingdom of heaven is at hand.' Heal the sick, cleanse the lepers, raise the dead, cast out demons. Freely you have received, freely give.

Matthew 10:1-8

Another very important secret of Jesus' success was delegation. He didn't do the work all by

Himself, but entrusted His disciples with some of the work, teaching them how it is done. In like manner, you also need to learn to delegate some aspects of your work to others in order to succeed. Team work produces greater results than what one man can do. Delegation helps you achieve more within a shorter period, producing excellent results as well as teaching others how it is done.

Until his father-in-law told him of the need to delegate, Moses was a one-man squad leading the people through the wilderness. But the stress was too much for him and tired him out very quickly.

> *So Moses' father-in-law said to him,*
> *"The thing that you do is not good.*
> *Both you and these people who are*
> *with you will surely wear yourselves*
> *out. For this thing is too much for*
> *you; you are not able to perform it by*
> *yourself.*
> *Listen now to my voice; I will give*
> *you counsel, and God will be with*
> *you: Stand before God for the*

people, so that you may bring the difficulties to God. And you shall teach them the statutes and the laws, and show them the way in which they must walk and the work they must do.

Moreover you shall select from all the people able men, such as fear God, men of truth, hating covetousness; and place such over them to be rulers of thousands, rulers of hundreds, rulers of fifties, and rulers of tens. And let them judge the people at all times. Then it will be that every great matter they shall bring to you, but every small matter they themselves shall judge. So it will be easier for you, for they will bear the burden with you.

Exodus 18:17-22

Thank God Moses heeded Jethro's counsel for delegation. The result was unbeatable.

And Moses chose able men out of all Israel, and made them heads over the people: rulers of thousands, rulers of hundreds, rulers of fifties, and rulers of tens. So they judged the people at all times; the hard cases they brought to Moses, but they judged every small case themselves.

Exodus 18:25-26

Jesus Christ also employed delegation in His ministry, and that is why the gospel is still being preached today though Christ has returned to heaven and is seated at the right hand of God. He had taught His disciples how to preach and heal, which they continued after He was no longer with them.

In several places in the gospels we see Jesus sending out His disciples in twos ahead of Him into villages and cities that He would later visit (Mark 6:7-13; Luke 10:1; Matthew 10:1). They went and the people were saved, delivered and healed, just as though it was Jesus. They were training on the job and were getting results. The difficult ones Jesus handled and taught them how it was done (Mark 9:14-29).

- **Trust In No Man**

Jesus loved everyone but He did not put His trust in any man. Rather, He trusted absolutely in the Father.

> *But Jesus did not commit Himself to them, because He knew all men, and had no need that anyone should testify of man, for He knew what was in man.*
>
> John 2:24-25

> *Do not put your trust in princes, nor in a son of man, in whom there is no help. His spirit departs, he returns to his earth; in that very day his plans perish.*
>
> Psalm 146:3-4

Jesus learnt not to put His trust in man. Yes, He worked with man; but trusted only in God. That was another secret for His success. Man is not reliable, he is like grass that is today and by tomorrow is no more. Man is naturally selfish, unstable and limited; putting your trust in man is to jeopardize your success.

> *Thus says the LORD: "Cursed is the man who trusts in man and makes flesh his strength, whose heart departs from the LORD. For he shall be like a shrub in the desert, and shall not see when good comes, but shall inhabit the parched places in the wilderness, in a salt land which is not inhabited.*
>
> Jeremiah 17:5-6

This definitely spells failure, and Jesus wanted to succeed. Since He was the word of God and knew the Father's will, He stayed clear of trusting in man. To put your trust in man is to sign-in for failure.

Jesus put all His trust in God, Who is forever stable, reliable, unlimited and a promise-keeper. God is answerable to no man and depends on nobody for His operations. This is what you get when you put your trust in God, rather than in man:

> *"Blessed is the man who trusts in the LORD, and whose hope is the LORD.*
> *For he shall be like a tree planted by the waters, which spreads out its roots by the river, and will not fear when heat comes; but its leaf will be green, and will not be anxious in the year of drought, nor will cease from yielding fruit.*

Jeremiah 17:7-8

This certainly is success!

> *Therefore trust in the Lord with all your heart, and lean not on your own understanding; in all your ways acknowledge Him, and He shall direct your paths.*

Proverbs 3:5-6

Jesus Christ was and is truly a resounding success! He engaged in the above success secret, and the success of His earthly ministry knew no bounds. His success is still speaking today and multiplying even though He is no more physically here on earth. You too can learn to put your trust absolutely in God, and enjoy success in life.

The Help of the Holy Spirit

The Holy Spirit played a very prominent role in Jesus' life and ministry. In fact, the success of Jesus' ministry can also be attributed to the helps of the Holy Spirit that He enjoyed. The Holy Spirit is the administrator of God's will on earth and so is the best authority to consult in all issues concerning your life. His impact on Christ's mission on earth cannot be overlooked and so must be mentioned and discussed.

> *How God anointed Jesus of Nazareth with the Holy Spirit and with power, who went about doing good and healing all who were oppressed by the devil, for God was with Him.*
>
> Acts 10:38

For He whom God has sent speaks the words of God, for God does not give the Spirit by measure.

John 3:34

And being assembled together with them, He commanded them not to depart from Jerusalem, but to wait for the Promise of the Father, "which," He said, "you have heard from Me;

But you shall receive power when the Holy Spirit has come upon you; and you shall be witnesses to Me in Jerusalem, and in all Judea and Samaria, and to the end of the earth."

Acts 1:4, 8

Jesus started and ended on earth successfully purely by the help of the Holy Spirit. The Godhead was the master-mind behind redemption: God the Father, God the Son and God the Holy Spirit (the Trinity). God the Father planned redemption

82

(Genesis 3:15), God the Son (Jesus) executed it (Matthew 1:21), and God the Holy Spirit will bring it to completion (Ephesians 4:30).

Long before the birth of Jesus Christ, the Holy Spirit through the prophets prophesied all about His birth, mission, crucifixion, death and resurrection (2 Peter 1:21; Isaiah 9:6-7; 52:13-53:12; Zechariah 12:10; Psalm 16:8-11; 22:1-31). The Holy Spirit started with Jesus from the very beginning, continued with Him till He departed the earth, and remained on earth to perfect the redemption agenda. He continued with Jesus' disciples and is still helping believers today.

- **Jesus' Conception**

Jesus was born of the Holy Spirit.

> *And the angel answered and said to her, "The Holy Spirit will come upon you, and the power of the Highest will overshadow you; therefore, also, that Holy One who is to be born will be called the Son of God.* Luke 1:35

Jesus the Son of God was conceived by the Holy Spirit, was born, grew and became strong in the Spirit (Luke 2:40).

- **Jesus' Baptism**

The Holy Spirit was present at Jesus' baptism also.

> *When He had been baptized, Jesus came up immediately from the water; and behold, the heavens were opened to Him, and He saw the Spirit of God descending like a dove and alighting upon Him.*
>
> *And suddenly a voice came from heaven, saying, "This is My beloved Son, in whom I am well pleased."*

Matthew 3:16-17

Jesus was ushered fully into ministry with His baptism by immersion and in the Holy Spirit. John the Baptist testified that God gave Christ the Spirit without measure, thereby empowering Him to fulfill His mission on earth (John 3:34).

Confirming the importance of the baptism in the Holy Spirit for success in life and ministry, Jesus commanded His disciples to remain in Jerusalem till they were baptized in the Holy Spirit, so they too can fulfill their ministry (Acts 1:4, 8).

- **Jesus' Temptation**

Being filled with the Spirit of God after the baptism, Jesus was led by the Spirit into the wilderness to prepare for His ministry. He spent forty days there, and was at the end tempted by the devil (Luke 4:1-15). Jesus was able, by the help of the Holy Spirit to resist every form of temptation the enemy brought His way - the lust of the flesh, the lust of the eyes and the pride of life (1 John 2:15-17).

At the end of the temptation, the Lord returned full of the power of the Holy Spirit into Galilee. News of Him spread around and people glorified Him as He taught in their synagogues.

- **His Ministry**

The Holy Spirit was of great help to Jesus in His ministry. When Jesus went into a synagogue in Nazareth, His home place, He was given the scriptures to read. He read from the book of Isaiah, and began to read:

> *"The Spirit of the Lord is upon Me, because He has anointed Me to preach the gospel to the poor; He has sent Me to heal the brokenhearted, to proclaim liberty to the captives and recovery of sight to the blind, to set at liberty those who are oppressed; to proclaim the acceptable year of the Lord."*

> Luke 4:18-19

At the end of His reading, Jesus declared to the people, *"Today this Scripture is fulfilled in your hearing."* The Holy Spirit upon Jesus is what empowered Him to do all that He did. Peter confirmed the fulfillment of this prophecy when he testified in Acts 10:38, that God anointed Jesus of Nazareth with the Holy Spirit, causing Him to go about doing good and healing all who were oppressed by the devil.

In response to accusations by the Pharisees that He was casting out demons by Beelzebub, Jesus inferred that He cast out demons by the Spirit of God and then warned that anyone who spoke against the Holy spirit would never be forgiven (Matthew 12:24-32).

Jesus was both full of the Holy Spirit and helped by the Holy Spirit. Even the words He spoke were filled with the Spirit.

> *It is the Spirit who gives life; the flesh profits nothing. The words that I speak to you are spirit, and they are life.*

> John 6:63

You too, like Jesus, can use the help of the Holy Spirit. He is the Spirit of God, and so knows the mind of the Father. He can reveal it to you, so you can live a victorious life operating by divine secrets.

• Jesus' Crucifixion

Death by crucifixion was the most shameful form of death in Jesus' days (Philippians 2:8; Galatians

3:13). It was disgraceful and the most dreaded method of execution. It is a slow, prolonged and painful execution in which the victim is tied or nailed to a large wooden cross and left to hang there until he dies. Before being crucified, Jesus was scourged to the point that He was too weak to carry His cross. They had to make Simon of Cyrene help Him (Matthew 27:32).

Jesus suffered all these for no crime of His! This brings to mind the scripture in Zechariah 4:6, which says that it is not by might nor by power, but by the Spirit of God. The Holy Spirit having shed the love of God for humanity in Christ's heart (Romans 5:5), enabled Him to suffer this type of humiliating death for the sins of mankind. On the cross, Jesus took your place and that of the whole world as a sinner and paid with His blood the price that we could not pay, all by the help of the Spirit of the Lord.

- **Resurrection**

The word of God clearly states that God the Father by His Spirit raised Jesus from the dead (Romans

8:11; Galatians 1:1). The Holy Spirit, the power of God and administrator of His will here on earth, was there on the third day to raise Jesus from the dead, as the prophets and Jesus had said (Luke 24:6-7).

Jesus' resurrection was the completion of God's salvation plan for man. If Christ had not risen from death, our faith would have been in vain, and we would still have remained in our sins (1 Corinthians 15:17). But praise God that Jesus arose from the dead by the power of the Holy Spirit!

• **Ascension**

The ascension of Jesus marked a new wave and reign of the Holy Spirit. Before Christ's crucifixion He said to His disciples in John 16:7:

> *Nevertheless I tell you the truth. It is to your advantage that I go away; for if I do not go away, the Helper will not come to you; but if I depart, I will send Him to you.*

Before Jesus' time, in the Old Testament, the Spirit of God only came upon kings, priests, prophets and a few people chosen for specific assignments. The Spirit of God was around people, but not within them. But on the day of Pentecost, the Spirit came upon the disciples and filled all of them (Acts 2:1-4); and has dwelt inside anyone that is baptized with the Spirit of God ever since.

As Jesus has said, we who believe in Him can now do the works that He did, and even greater works than He did, by the help of the Holy Spirit that dwells within us (John 14:12). Jesus didn't operate independently of the Holy Spirit. His success in ministry is fully attributed to the work of the Spirit of God that was with and in Him. If Christ couldn't do without the Holy Spirit, be sure that you can't do without Him. No one can have a successful life or ministry without the Holy Spirit working in him or her. He is our Helper sent from the Father, use Him!

Chapter Three

Jesus and His Words

An understanding of the gospel of Jesus Christ has made it easier for me to live as a Christian. Not that I have arrived; but by the help of the Holy Spirit, following the words of Christ has kept me thus far as a believer in Christ and is delivering God's blessings to me as He has promised. Whenever I obey and walk by faith in line with Christ's words written in the Bible, I always get my desires from God. Sometimes the answer comes immediately, and some other times after a period of time; but the answer surely do come.

Christ is His words and His words are Him. You can't separate Jesus from His words. No wonder, the world was both formed and maintained by His words (John 1:1-3; Hebrews 1:3). An understanding and practice of Jesus' words and truths will give you victory in all aspects of life.

In this chapter, therefore, we will learn the main focus of Christ's messages and how to use His words in order to enjoy continuous breakthroughs in life.

The Greatest Commandment

What do you think is the greatest commandment? Jesus pointed out the two great commands of God, and went on towards the end of His mission to give His disciples a new commandment. The summary of these three commands is the core of the new covenant.

> *Jesus said to him, "You shall love the Lord your God with all your heart, with all your soul, and with all your mind.' This is the first and great commandment. And the second is like it: 'You shall love your neighbor as yourself.' On these two commandments hang all the Law and the Prophets."*

> Matthew 22:37-40

> *I give you a new commandment: that you should love one another. Just as*

I have loved you, so you too should love one another.

John 13:34 (AMP)

Many people emphasize the importance of the Ten Commandments, and they should. But the truth is that following the three great commandments of Jesus fully takes care of the Ten Commandments. In the Old Testament if you break one commandment you have broken all (James 2:10), but in the New Testament when you obey the three commands of Jesus, you will automatically obey all the Old Testament Ten Commandments. What are these three commandments?

1. Love God with all your being

Jesus said that this is the first and great commandment. You are to love God with all your heart, soul and mind. This means that God is to be number one on your priority list; every other thing should come after God. To love God is to obey all His commandments, including the Ten

Commandments. God is to dictate your thoughts, words and actions. In summary, breathe God!

2. Love your neighbour as yourself

Jesus described this as the second commandment, and James calls it the royal law (James 2:8). You are to love your neighbour as you love yourself. What you won't like done to you, don't do to anyone else. Doing this command will take care of the sixth to tenth laws in the Ten Commandments: thou shall not kill, commit adultery, steal, bear false witness against your neighbour and covet his/her things. If you love your neighbour you will not do any of these evils to him/her. Instead, you will cherish and protect him/her as you would yourself.

3. Love the brethren

Jesus called this a new commandment, and it is addressed specifically to Christians (followers of Christ).

By this all will know that you are My disciples, if you have love for one another."

John 13:35

Loving the brethren as Jesus loves us is how the world will know that we are disciples of Jesus. We are the epistles the world reads about Christ (2 Corinthians 3:2-3). By loving one another we show the world the love of God, which should attract them to Jesus. They would want to have what we have, which is Jesus. This commandment glories God. But when there is strife, bitterness and hatred in the Church, we fail and dishonour God.

The success of your Christian faith lies in your obedience to these commandments of Jesus. Walking in love is very important to God. That is why He gave us the Holy Spirit, Who has shed God's love abroad in our hearts, so we can easily obey God's laws and commandment. Whoever loves knows God, for God is love (1 John 4:8). God's commandments are not burdensome (1 John 5:3), so strive to walk in the love of God always.

Jesus' Gospel

What is Jesus' gospel? What is Jesus known for? You will understand and appreciate the Lord more when you know the basis of His teachings. God sent Jesus to the world with a message for the liberation of mankind.

> *For God so loved the world that He gave His only begotten Son, that whoever believes in Him should not perish but have everlasting life.*
>
> John 3:16
>
> *And the Word became flesh and dwelt among us, and we beheld His glory, the glory as of the only begotten of the Father, full of grace and truth...*
>
> *And of His fullness we have all received, and grace for grace. For the law was given through Moses, but grace and truth came through Jesus Christ.*
>
> John 1:14-17

He who did not spare His own Son, but delivered Him up for us all, how shall He not with Him also freely give us all things?

Romans 8:32

Jesus Christ preached the gospel of the love and grace of God. Jesus came with a message of love and grace. These two ingredients will change the life of anyone who receives them, as they make it easy for one to live a victorious life on earth. Before Jesus came, man was struggling to obey God, defeat the devices of the enemy and enjoy life all at once. This was practically impossible without any help. Jesus' coming to the world brought a message of hope and victory for man.

• The Gospel Of God's Love

Jesus came to show the world God's love. The heart of man is deceitful and desperately wicked (Jeremiah 17:9), and so is incapable of loving anyone selflessly. This made it almost impossible for man to relate well with one another. It should be noted that this was not man's original nature.

Man was created in God's image and possessed God's nature until sin came in through Adam and corrupted him.

God's love for man moved Him to send Jesus to the world, to help man out of his predicament (John 3:16). Jesus died on the cross bearing all of man's sins, and arose from the dead for the redemption of man. Jesus came to give His life for the ransom of many (Matthew 20:28). While here on earth, Jesus preached and showed us the love of God. We can now love God and man because God first loved us (1 John 4:19).

> *He who did not spare His own Son, but delivered Him up for us all, how shall He not with Him also freely give us all things?*
>
> Romans 8:32

The above verse reveals the depth of God's love for man. Not only has He given us Jesus, He will also freely give us all things! Jesus came to reveal the Father God of love to humanity.

Before Jesus came, the world only knew Him as the God of judgement. In the Old Testament it was an eye for an eye, and a tooth for a tooth. But God's love now teaches us to turn the other cheek for another slap. It is no longer okay to merely love your friend but hate your enemy; we are now commanded to love our enemies as well, bless those who curse us, and do good to those who hate you (Matthew 5:38-48).

"Is this not weakness?" you might ask. No; rather, it is great strength! It takes a lot of strength and boldness to be able to love anyone with the love of God. He who loves like this is superior to the one receiving the love. Christ showed us an example to follow in that while we were yet sinners, He who knew no sin died for us (Romans 5:8; 2 Corinthians 5:21).

Imagine what the world would be like if humanity loves like God does! We would all enjoy abundant peace! The good news is that you can increase the effect of God's love by choosing to love like God loves and Jesus exemplified. Tremendous power is emitted when you love others with the love of Christ. Many of the miracles Jesus performed were preceded by His being moved with compassion for the recipients. For example, moved with compassion on seeing the great multitude, Jesus healed their sick (Matthew 14:14).

The love of God at work in Christ was what made Him ask the Father to forgive His crucifiers while still on the cross (Luke 23:34). Today, Jesus' love for man, which drove Him to the cross, has redeemed and restored many back to God! Now, many sons have been raised to glory by His love and sacrifice!

God is showing us through Jesus' gospel that we can achieve more by loving others with His kind of love. We will live longer and prosper more by loving like Jesus. In addition, victory over sin would become a reality when we love with the love of the Lord (1 Corinthians 13:4-8), and the world would be a better place to live in.

- **The Gospel of God's Grace**

  Knowing that man would struggle with "loving like Christ", God also sent Jesus with the message of grace. While the law was given through Moses, grace and truth came through Jesus Christ (John 1:17). Jesus came full of grace, and of His fullness have we all received grace (John 1:14-16).

The grace of God is the unearned, undeserved favour and spiritual blessing of God (John 1:17 [AMP]). Grace is also God working in you, through you and with you to achieve a task. The grace of God enables you to enjoy all that redemption has to offer, as well as helps you to do or achieve what could have been impossible if you were simply relying on your abilities.

Jesus operated by the grace of God here on earth. God's grace was upon Him at birth (Luke 2:40) and by that same grace He went to the cross and died the most shameful death in order for us to be saved from our sins (Hebrews 2:9). Jesus started and successfully completed His assignment on the earth by the grace of God.

God's grace makes His power and ability available to you. It puts you over negative situations. Believers are saved by grace and can only overcome by grace (Ephesians 2:8). A life of holiness and righteous can only be possible by the grace of God, because God is at work in you both to will and to do of His good pleasure (Philippians 2:13). It would no more be by your power or might, but by the helps of the Holy Spirit that lives in you (Zechariah 4:6). Only the grace of God can make you love people with the love of God.

Paul, a great apostle of Christ, attributed his success in ministry to the grace of God at work in him.

> ***But by the grace of God I am what I am, and His grace toward me was not in vain; but I labored more abundantly than they all, yet not I, but the grace of God which was with me.*** 1 Corinthians 15:10

All of Paul's exploits in ministry was done by the grace of God. When he was faced with a great challenge, for which he prayed to God for, God's response to him was grace.

> *Concerning this thing I pleaded with the Lord three times that it might depart from me. And He said to me, "My grace is sufficient for you, for My strength is made perfect in weakness." Therefore most gladly I will rather boast in my infirmities, that the power of Christ may rest upon me.*

2 Corinthians 12:8-9

The gospel of Jesus is loaded with great blessings enveloped by the love of God and delivered to us by the grace of God. God's love and grace compels Him to bless us and give us His best (Romans 8:32). All of God's blessings come to us by His grace, because we often don't deserve them and can't earn them. They are purely His spiritual blessings which He delivers to us through Christ.

Jesus and Persecution

Have you ever wondered what the right response to persecution should be? What would Jesus do if He were the one being persecuted? You don't need to guess the answer, because Jesus told us what our response should be. He was also persecuted, and so left us examples to follow.

> *But I say to you, love your enemies, bless those who curse you, do good to those who hate you, and pray for those who spitefully use you and persecute you,*
>
> Matthew 5:44

> *So he answered and said to me: "This is the word of the Lord to Zerubbabel: 'Not by might nor by power, but by My Spirit,' says the Lord of hosts.*
>
> Zechariah 4:6

Many face persecutors often, if not daily, and are getting weary of them; they are probably wondering the right response to them should be without disobeying God. The scriptures admonish us to look unto Jesus, the author and finisher of our faith (Hebrews 12:2). Follow His steps and you will not miss the way.

Jesus' Response

Jesus had so many persecutors when He was on earth, and even till now; but He had one response to them all - to pray for them. "What! Is that all?" Yes, Christ said you should pray for those that spitefully use and persecute you (Matthew 5:44). He also showed us examples to follow.

For instance, at the garden of Gethsemane, when the soldiers came to arrest Jesus on the orders of His persecutors, He didn't support one of His disciples who cut off the ear of a servant of the high priest; He rather rebuked him. He told Peter that if He needed to, He could have asked His Father to send Him more than twelve legions of angels (who excel in strength) to take care of His enemies (Matthew 26:51-53). The climax of Christ's response to His persecutors came when

He prayed for them on the cross. Instead of calling down fire to devour His enemies, He asked God to forgive them; that they knew not what they were doing!

You may be wondering, "Why would Jesus respond like this?" My response would be because it is not the will of the Father that anyone should perish, but that all should come to repentance (2 Peter 3:9). Besides, the highest persecutors can do is to kill the body. But if they don't repent from their sins, God in heaven will both destroy their bodies and souls in hell (Matthew 10:28).

How possible is it to follow Jesus' example in dealing with our persecutors? Well, one thing for sure is that Jesus never gives us instructions that are impossible to obey, for His yoke is easy to bear and His burden is light (Matthew 11:30). The Bible also tells us that His commandments are not grievous (1 John 5:3). You should know that God will not allow you to be tempted above what you are able to bear. Instead, He will make a way of escape for you from the temptation, so you can bear it (1 Corinthians 10:13).

In addition, you can do all things, including praying for your persecutors, through Christ who strengthens you (Philippians 4:13). In fact, overcoming persecution is actually not by your might or power, but by the help of the Holy Spirit that dwells in you.

A Human Example

Stephen is a good example of someone who did exactly what Jesus did. He was persecuted to the point of death; but rather than curse those who spitefully used him, he prayed for them like his master Jesus did.

> *Then he knelt down and cried out with a loud voice, "Lord, do not charge them with this sin." And when he had said this, he fell asleep.*
>
> Acts 7:60

Paul commands us to *"Bless those who persecute you; bless and do not curse"* (Romans 12:14).

Another thing that may be going through your mind is, "For how long should they be allowed to persecute me?" The Bible tells us that love suffers long (1 Corinthians 13:4). But let me assure you that there is a limit to their oppression; it won't last long or forever. Your duty is to pray that they repent and that God would bless them. How God would do that is His business; leave it to Him. You can also ask God to deliver you from them. God will certainly avenge His own children, who cry day and night to Him, though He may bear long with your persecutors (Luke 18:7).

A typical case in point was what happened to King Herod in Acts 12:20-23. Herod had harassed some from the Church. He had killed James the brother of John, and had picked on Peter as his next victim. The disciples, however, prayed to God to deliver Peter from his hands. God answered their prayers and miraculously delivered Peter from prison on the night before his execution. Then God finally judged the king when he failed to give Him all the glory. An angel of the Lord struck him, and he was eaten up by worms and died on the spot.

Jesus is love and stands for love. He, for love sake suffered long that men may be saved. God the Father also for love sake gave His only Son, that whosoever believes in Him will not perish but have everlasting life (John 3:16). Love says you should bless those that curse you, and pray for those who persecute you. When you do this, God will surely deliver you from their hands. If they choose not to repent, but continue in their evil, God's wrath and judgement will certainly come upon them.

A Word for Quick Turnaround

Have you been toiling long with nothing to show for it? Do you desire a quick turnaround in life? One word from Jesus is what you need for a turnaround! A wise man once said that one word of encounter is worth much more than many years of effort.

The centurion answered and said, "Lord, I am not worthy that You should come under my roof. But only <u>speak a word</u>, and my servant will be healed...

Then Jesus said to the centurion, "Go your way; and as you have believed, so let it be done for you." And his servant was healed that same hour.

Matthew 8:8, 13 (emphasis mine)

When He had stopped speaking, He said to Simon, "Launch out into the deep and let down your nets for a catch."

But Simon answered and said to Him, "Master, we have <u>toiled all night</u> and caught nothing; <u>nevertheless at Your word</u> I will let down the net." And when they had done this, they caught a great

number of fish, and their net was
breaking.

Luke 5:4-6 (emphasis mine)

You may have prayed, fasted, made all the right confessions, and even worked very hard, and yet seem to have gotten nothing in return for your effort, and you are now asking, "What haven't I done?" The answer is that you have not gotten a word from Jesus yet! His word makes all the difference, as the above scriptures reveal.

A word from Jesus commands prompt actions from whatever or wherever He sends it.

So shall My word be that goes forth
from My mouth; it shall not return to
Me void, but it shall accomplish what
I please, and it shall prosper in the
thing for which I sent it.

Isaiah 55:11

Everything in heaven, on earth and beneath the earth bows to His commands. They can never resist His words. Do you wonder why? Jesus Christ co-created the world and everything within it with God the Father and the Holy Spirit (Genesis 1:26; John 1:1-3). As a result, everything is subject to Him; He is Lord over all. The centurion in Matthew 8:8-9 understood this. He considered that if he, being a man under authority, can command obedience from the people under him, Jesus Christ would be able to command more from all His subjects.

What are those things subject to Jesus? Every authority, power, dominion and anything that has a name, whether in the spiritual or physical world, is subject to Jesus (Ephesians 1:20-21). Everything means everything, with no exceptions. This is why demons, sickness and diseases, earth, trees, water and even death obey Jesus.

Christ's words are powerful and are able to deliver your desired turnaround, and quickly too. One word from Jesus will cause situations to change instantly. Peter, a seasoned fisherman, had an encounter with Jesus and His word, and experienced a net-breaking, boat-sinking turnaround (Luke 5:1-9). Peter and his fishing

112

colleagues had toiled all night long (which, by the way, is the best time for fishing) and caught nothing. But when a word came from Jesus to launch out into the deep and let down their nets in broad day light for a draught, all the fishes in that sea gathered from everywhere to their nets. They caught a great multitude of fishes that their nets began to break. They had to beckon on other fishermen to come to their rescue. What a catch! Truly, all you need is just a word from Jesus.

In the story of the marriage in Cana of Galilee, we see another example of what an encounter with Jesus' words can do (John 2:1-10). When wine was running out at the marriage ceremony, Mary, Jesus' mother, told the servants, "Whatsoever He says unto you, do it." That was the secret that averted shame. When the servants obeyed Jesus' command to fill the water pots with water, He instructed that they drew from the pot and take to the master of the feast. Water was turned into the best wine ever tasted on their way to the master of the feast! That is what I call quick turnaround!

How can you get these words for your own quick turnaround? You need to continue in the scriptural steps you have been taking: word study, fasting and praying and right confessions, etc. In addition, however, you must create time to listen for the Master's voice. You need to be sensitive in the spirit and tune your spiritual ears to hear Jesus when He speaks to you. Jesus is always speaking to us. The problem is that we are more conscious of physical things and the world than the spiritual, and so our ears are not well tuned to hear Him.

It is wisdom to spend time to hear from Jesus concerning that situation, if you desire a change for the better. Don't be in a haste to take steps. One word encounter will save you hours, days, months and even years of wasted effort, frustration and terminal occurrences.

How to Trigger Jesus' Words

One word from Jesus is worth much more than years of toiling. Just one word from Him will bring about that much-needed turnaround. How then can you trigger His word for a change in your situation?

> *Then He got into one of the boats, which was Simon's, and asked him to put out a little from the land. And He sat down and taught the multitudes from the boat.*
> *When He had stopped speaking, He said to Simon, "Launch out into the deep and let down your nets for a catch."*
>
> Luke 5:3-4

> *And he said to him, "Say now to her, 'Look, you have been concerned for us with all this care. What can I do for you? Do you want me to speak on your behalf to the king or to the commander of the army? She answered, "I dwell among my own people."*
>
> 2 Kings 4:13

For God is not unjust to forget your work and labor of love which you have shown toward His name, in that you have ministered to the saints, and do minister.

Hebrews 6:10

Simply put, let Jesus use what you have! That is the simplest way to provoke Him to speak a word for your turnaround. When you release yourself or what you have for the sake of the kingdom of God, you provoke Him to release a blessing on you through His words. God is not a user of men, but a rewarder of them that diligently seek Him (Hebrews 11:6). There is nothing you do for the promotion of God's kingdom that ever goes unnoticed. Every seed sown in the name of Jesus Christ must bear bountiful harvest.

Peter in Luke 5:1-11 triggered Jesus' word for a quick turnaround when he made his boat available to Jesus to sit in and teach the multitude. The Shunammite woman triggered God's word via His servant Elisha when she made her home, money and food available to the man of God (2 Kings 4:8-17). Though she was rich and influential, she had no child. Her hospitality provoked the word of the Lord through Elisha: *"About this time next year you shall embrace a son."*

Acts chapter 10 tells the story of Cornelius, a centurion who feared God, gave alms generously to people and prayed always. One day, he saw a vision of an angel telling him that those actions had come before God as a memorial. Cornelius was then instructed to send for Peter, who would tell him what he must do. By his service to the kingdom, Cornelius and his household received salvation, and were the first set of gentiles upon whom the Holy Ghost fell.

In contemporary times, there are countless testimonies of people who gave their homes for house fellowships, vehicles to transport people to church or for the promotion of the gospel, their lands and properties for the kingdom work, and their time, energy and money for the propagation of the gospel of Christ. Doing these things for the kingdom sake has brought about bountiful change of story for them in return. Many were healed of sicknesses and diseases, others had financial breakthroughs, some conceived after many years of barrenness, while yet others had their debts cancelled.

Giving yourself and what you have to Christ and the kingdom is sure to trigger the release of a word from Jesus, which will in turn cause a quick turnaround in your life and situation. Therefore, look inwards and around you for that thing that will provoke the release of the word. Allow the Holy Spirit to guide you.

Let me sound a word of caution here. Don't give to the kingdom primarily because of what you anticipate to get from God. It is best to give because you love Him and you want the kingdom work to prosper. All the examples I cited earlier gave without expecting anything in return. But because God is not unjust to forget our work and labour of love, He released the words that brought about their desired change. I see Christ releasing

His words for your quick turnaround as you let Him use you and what you have today, in Jesus' name!

Chapter Four

Life in Jesus

But these are written that you may believe that Jesus is the Christ, the Son of God, and that believing <u>you may have life</u> in His name.

John 20:31

How is your life now? Are you enjoying it or merely enduring it? Would you recommend the kind of life you have now to someone else? Life can really be exciting if you have the right foundation.

Life without Jesus Christ is a life filled with crisis. This is because life is much more than possessions of wealth, position or power. Some have all these and more, and still live miserable lives. Some of them even commit suicide in spite of all the worldly goods they have. Meanwhile, there are some others who may not possess too much riches and power, but are actually enjoying their lives.

What could be their secret? It is a life in Jesus Christ.

Having Jesus Christ as your Lord and Saviour is the greatest gift you can have in life. Jesus is the right foundation to build upon. Possessing Jesus first and then other goodies is what make life enjoyable.

What does a life lived in Jesus Christ look like? What should one expect? This chapter is focused on showing what life in Jesus Christ is like.

Signs, Wonders and Lessons

Life in Jesus is a life filled with signs, wonders and miracles. Every miracle is purely by the finger of God, including those performed by Jesus. Jesus Christ performed great and diverse miracles, including healing multitudes of people. No sick person that came to Him for healing returned sick; they all received their healing!

> *And when the Sabbath had come, He began to teach in the synagogue. And many hearing Him were*

astonished, saying, "Where did this Man get these things? And what wisdom is this which is given Him, that such mighty works are performed by His hands!

Mark 6:2

I can of Myself do nothing. As I hear, I judge; and My judgment is righteous, because I do not seek My own will but the will of the Father who sent Me.

John 5:30

The miracles were so great that the people could not help but wonder where He got the wisdom from. But amazingly, Jesus gave the glory to the Father, saying He couldn't have done any of them without God.

Which of Jesus' miracles do you remember? What lessons did you glean from them, and which ones have you applied to your life? Whatever miracle Jesus performed can happen for you as well if you so desire. Below are some of the miracles He performed and lessons that can be drawn from them.

> ### Water Turned Into Wine – John 2:1-12

Jesus was a guest at a wedding in Cana of Galilee. His mother and disciples were also guests at the wedding. They ran out of wine at the wedding, and Jesus' mother told Him about it, expecting Him to do something about it. Though Jesus initially seemed uninterested in the matter, that didn't dissuade His mother, who told the servants to do whatever Jesus tells them to do.

Jesus instructed them to fill the water pots with water, and they did. He then told them to draw some out and take it to the master of the feast, and they again obeyed Him. Apparently, as they were going to the master of the feast, the water miraculously turned into wine. This, the master of the feast confirmed, as he declared it good wine. This was Christ's first miracle.

Lessons:

- Never forget to invite Jesus to whatever you are doing.

- If you encounter any challenge don't hesitate to tell it to Him.
- Always do whatever He tells you to do, even if it sounds foolish.
- Jesus is never late, and His things are always the best.

➤ The Nobleman's Son Healed – John 4:46-54

A certain nobleman whose son was sick to the point of death at Capernaum heard that Jesus was in town. He went to Jesus, imploring Him to come and heal his son. Rather than go with the man to his house, Jesus told him to go his way, that his son was alive. The nobleman believed Jesus and went home. He was met on the way by his servants, who told him that his son was healed. He asked when the boy got better, and discovered it was the same time that Jesus had told him his son was alive. As a result, he and his household believed in Christ.

Lessons:

- Seek Jesus wherever you can find Him.

- You are free to ask Him whatever you desire.

- Believe every word that Jesus speaks to you, even if it's not what you expected to hear from Him or what you desired Him to say or do.

- Christ's ways are higher and better than our ways.

- God's goodness brings about repentance.

➢ The Feeding Of The Multitudes – John 6:1-14; Matthew 15:32-39

In John 6:1-14, a great multitude, including about five thousand men, followed Jesus over the sea of Galilee. When Jesus saw the multitude He asked Philip where they could buy bread to feed the people, testing Philip, for Jesus already knew what He would do. Philip answered Him that two hundred denarii's worth of bread would not be sufficient for them to have even a bite.

Andrew came along to inform them that a lad had five barley loaves and two small fishes, but wondered what that could do among so many people. Jesus instructed His disciples to make the people sit down. He then took the loaves and fish, gave thanks and handed them to His disciples, who passed it on to the people. The people ate, were filled, and had left overs! The left over from five loaves and two small fishes filled twelve baskets! Amazed, the people declared that Jesus was truly the Prophet who was to come into the world.

A similar incidence happened in Matthew 15:32-39. Jesus needed to feed four thousand men, besides women and children, after three days of having eaten nothing. They had only seven loaves and a few little fish. Jesus took these, broke it and gave it to His disciples to distribute to the people. They too ate and were filled, and the disciples gathered seven large baskets as left overs!

Lessons:

- Jesus Christ is always concerned about our welfare.

- Sometimes, God may test you to know how much faith you have and how much you know Him.

- Whatever you have is enough for God to work with.

- Christ is very orderly and organized (He always made them sit down in groups). You should be also.

- Thanksgiving is a key to multiplication.

- Team work is essential for success in life.

- Jesus hates wastes; accountability is an important quality to possess.

> **Lazarus Raised From Death – John 11:1-44**

When Lazarus of Bethany, brother to Mary and Martha was sick, his sisters sent a message to Jesus that he was sick. When Jesus heard it He quickly declared that the sickness was not unto death, but for the glory of God. However, He stayed two more days in the place where He was, before He and His disciples left to see Lazarus.

Lazarus had been dead and buried in the tomb four days before Jesus arrived. After an insightful discussion with Martha, Jesus requested to be shown Lazarus' tomb. The people around wondered why Jesus who opened blind eyes could not keep the sick Lazarus from dying.

On getting to the tomb, Jesus asked that the stone placed at the entrance be removed. Martha reminded him that by now there would be a great stench, as Lazarus had been dead four days. Jesus reminded her of what He had told her earlier, that if she only believed, she would see the glory of God. When the stone was removed, Jesus lifted up His eyes and thanked God the Father. Then in a loud voice He called forth Lazarus from the dead, and he who was dead came out bound hand and foot with grave-clothes. Jesus said to them, "Loose him and let him go."

Lessons:

- God hears you at the time you pray to Him in faith.

- Declaring what you want in the face of a contrary situation empowers your desire to come to pass.

- God is never late.

- God will not always act as you expect.

- There is no situation too smelly, messy, difficult or impossible that God cannot intervene in to put a smile on your face.

- If you can believe, you will see the glory of God in that situation.

- Every stone blocking your freedom or deliverance needs to be removed before you can come forth: it could be the stone of unbelief or doubt, disobedience, un-forgiveness, etc.

- Your salvation is not with man but with God, so look up to Jesus.

- Thanksgiving unto God is a vital step for your victory to be delivered.
- Jesus always finishes His work on you. He is not done until you are loosed and free to go.

➢ Tribute Money From A Fish – Matthew 17:24-27

At Capernaum, temple tax collectors asked Peter if Jesus paid temple taxes, and Peter answered yes. As soon as Peter entered the house, without having been told anything, Jesus asked Peter who the kings of the earth took taxes from, their sons or strangers.

> *Peter said to Him, "From strangers."*
> *Jesus said to him, "Then the sons are free.*
> *Nevertheless, lest we offend them, go to the sea, cast in a hook, and take the fish that comes up first. And when you have opened its mouth, you will find a piece of money; take*

that and give it to them for Me and you."

Matthew 17:26-27

Lessons:

- God hears all our conversations.

- You should not always insist on your rights.

- You should obey authorities.

- God can bless you through any means, including from the mouth of a fish.

- God's provisions are always sufficient.

➢ **The Woman With The Issue Of Blood – Mark 5:25-34**

A certain woman had a flow of blood for twelve years. She had been to many physicians and spent all her life's savings, but didn't get better. When she heard that Jesus was coming to town, she determined to meet Him, in the hope of a cure. Before leaving home, she said within herself, "If only I can touch His garment, I shall be made whole."

So while others were trying to touch Jesus, she simply went for His garment; and as she had hoped for, she was healed immediately! Knowing that power had gone out of Him, Jesus turned around and asked, "Who touched My clothes?" His disciples were amazed at His question, seeing that He was being thronged by multitudes. When Jesus persisted with His question, the woman came forward, and told what had happened. Jesus concluded by saying to her, *"Daughter, your faith has made you well. Go in peace, and be healed of your affliction."*

Lessons:

- Jesus is the last bus stop for whatever challenge you are faced with. God will never refer you to any other physician; He has the answer to that problem.

- Your mouth is the gateway to your salvation: you shall have what you say.

- Christ is the cheapest consultant, as He charges nothing to help you. But He loves it when you receive Him as your Lord and Saviour.

- You need to take immediate action with the message of Christ that you hear, so you can access your blessings from God.
- Your faith makes you well.

➤ Jesus Walks On Water – Matthew 14:22-33

After feeding the multitude, Jesus sent them home, sent His disciples to the other side in a ship ahead of Him, while He went to the mountain to pray. There was a storm at sea, and the ship the disciples were in was tossed by the waves. After praying, Jesus walked on the sea to join His disciples. On seeing someone walking on water towards them, they were all afraid. Jesus reassured them, saying to them, "Be of good cheer! It is I; do not be afraid."

Wanting to be very sure, Peter said if it was truly Jesus walking towards them, He should command him to join Him on the water, to which Jesus said,

"Come." Peter immediately got off the boat and actually began walking on water towards Jesus! But when he saw the boisterous wind, he became afraid and began to sink. He cried out to Jesus to save him. Jesus stretched out His hand and caught Peter, reproving him for his little faith. The wind ceased when they got into the boat. Amazed by what they had just witnessed, those in the boat came and worshipped Jesus, affirming that truly He was the Son of God.

Lessons:

- God's voice commands peace of mind, causing fear to disappear and be replaced with boldness.
- You will experience miracles when you act on God's words.
- Looking away from Jesus to the troubles before you will only bring more fear and sinking.

- No matter at what stage of life, Jesus will always stretch out His hands to save you when you call upon Him for help.
- Circumstances will always bow to the presence of God.
- Miracles will always stir up the worship of God in you.

➤ The Wind And Waves Obey Jesus – Mark 4:35-41

Jesus and His disciples decided to cross over to the other side by boat. However, half way through, a great windstorm arose and the waves beat into the boat, so much so that the boat was fast being filled with water. Meanwhile, Jesus was sound asleep in the midst of all the confusion and fear of drowning. In desperation, Jesus' disciples went to Him, saying, *"Teacher, do You not care that we are perishing?"*

Jesus arose and rebuked the wind. He said to the sea, *"Peace, be still!"* The wind ceased immediately, and there was a great calm. Then

Jesus said to them, "Why are you so fearful? How is it that you have no faith?" But the disciples wondered among themselves who He was, that even the wind and the sea obey Him.

Lessons:

- Jesus is the Prince of Peace. He offers all who will come to Him the peace that passes all understanding; the peace that will cause you to be at rest even in the midst of a fiery storm. This peace is available to all who will receive Him as their Lord and Saviour.

- Every created thing hears the words and voice of Jesus Christ and must obey Him.

- By faith in Jesus, all Christian believers can do the exact things Jesus did.

- Fear is a hindrance to the exploits we can do in Christ.

➢ The Healing Of The Ten Lepers – Luke 17:11-19

Jesus entered a certain village and met ten lepers. They cried out to him for mercy, and He asked them to go and show themselves to the priests. As they went, they were cleansed. One of them, a Samaritan, when he saw that he was healed returned to thank Jesus. Jesus asked for the other nine who didn't return to give glory to God. He then said to the Samaritan that returned, *"Arise, go your way. Your faith has made you well."*

Lessons:

- Jesus will never ignore a cry of mercy.
- Whatever Jesus tells you to do, do it, no matter how foolish it may sound.
- Your answer will come as you obey and do the instructions given you.
- It's important to always return to give God all the glory, because that is when your testimony is perfected.
- Your faith will always make you whole.

➢ The Healing Of A Centurion's Servant – Matthew 8:5-13

A centurion met Jesus in Capernaum and pleaded with Him to heal his sick servant. Jesus offered to go with the centurion, but the centurion said he was not worthy to have Jesus under his roof. Rather, he said Jesus should only speak a word and his servant at home would be healed. As a man under authority and one who had people under him, the centurion understood the role of commands and how they must be obeyed. He knew that Jesus' commands would be obeyed, no matter where it was issued from.

Jesus marveled at the centurion's words, describing it as great faith. He then said to the centurion, *"Go your way; and as you have believed, so let it be done for you."* The centurion's servant was healed the same hour Jesus gave the command, just as he had believed!

Lessons:

- Jesus Christ is always ready to heal.

- Jesus' words are full of authority and everyone and thing that hears them must obey Him.
- Great faith pleases God.
- It is to you according to your faith.
- It doesn't take God time to answer you; but your faith is what determines the speed with which you receive your answers.

These miracles were documented so we can learn from them and believe God to do the same in our lives. Jesus said in John 14:12:

> *"Most assuredly, I say to you, he who believes in Me, the works that I do he will do also; and greater works than these he will do…*

Are you ready for great works? They can happen for you and through you.

An Inheritance-Filled Life

Life in Jesus is a life filled with great inheritances and blessings. God, like the good Father that He is, has bestowed rich inheritances upon every child of His. Just as in the natural people strive to leave riches and property for their loved ones to enjoy after they are gone, Jesus has also left us great inheritances to enjoy here on earth.

- **Peace**

One of the inheritances you will enjoy in Christ is His peace.

> *These things I have spoken to you, that in Me you may have peace. In the world you will have tribulation; but be of good cheer, I have overcome the world."*

> John 16:33

> *Peace I leave with you, My peace I give to you; not as the world gives do I give to you. Let not your heart be troubled, neither let it be afraid.*

> John 14:27

In this world you are sure to have tribulations, but you will have peace if you are in Christ. The peace Jesus gives was what enabled Him to sleep soundly in the boat in spite of the storm (Mark 4:36-41), to walk on water (Matthew 14:25-33), and to remain calm in Gethsemane when He was being arrested (Matthew 26:47-56). He also manifested this peace at the tomb of Lazarus (John 11:38-44) and many other places in scriptures.

This has been my testimony. I have had my fair share of challenges in life; but I have also enjoyed the peace of God in spite of the challenges, because I have Jesus. Life in Christ is a life of righteous, peace and joy in the Holy Ghost. When others are saying there is a casting down for them, for me it has always been a lifting up. My soul is never downcast, for I know that Jesus has overcome the world already. He is more than able to see me through any challenge.

I also believe, like the Psalmist, that even if I walk through the valley of the shadow of death, I will fear no evil because Jesus is with me. His word (rod) and Spirit comforts me (Psalm 23:4). This is what life in Jesus is like.

Jesus' peace (His inheritance to us) is what you need in order to go through the storms of life. He is the Prince of peace; in Him alone can you find and have peace. Jesus already told us that the world is filled with tribulation, admonishing us to *"be of good cheer,"* for He has overcome the world (John 16:33). When others are saying there is a casting down, this peace is what will enable you say there is a lifting up instead.

All through His suffering and persecution that preceded His crucifixion, the Pharisees rejoiced, believing that His end had come. But Jesus was at peace because He knew His death would only end up as victory for Him and humanity. Jesus didn't bother to defend Himself before Pilate when the chief priests and elders falsely accused Him. He had so much peace that the governor marveled greatly (Matthew 27:12-14).

It is this kind of peace that Jesus has left us for an inheritance; so that we can unseat every devil around us and enjoy the blessings of redemption. He gave us His peace from the abundance that He possessed, for no one can give what he doesn't have.

- **Joy**

Joy is another benefit of living in Jesus Christ. It is not dependent on circumstances, but on God's love, supremacy and the infallibility of His word. You are ever joyful and bubbling come rain, come shine. To enjoy life is to be rejoicing all the time. This, you can only achieve when you are in Christ.

- **Righteousness**

Some desire to live a life without sin, but keep failing. At the beginning of every year they make New Year resolutions and fall short of them after a while. Only Jesus Christ can give you the power to overcome sin. It is practically impossible to live a righteous life without Christ, as righteousness comes freely with salvation (2 Corinthians 5:21; 1 John 3:6).

- **Security**

There are no complexities in a life in Christ, as a believer is secured in Jesus; he knows who he is as a child of God. There is also no fear in a life lived in Jesus Christ. Insecurity causes people to do all manner of foolish and evil things; but a believer is free to enjoy a life of security.

> *And you shall know the truth, and*
> *the truth shall make you free...*
> *Therefore if the Son makes you free,*
> *you shall be free indeed.*
>
> John 8:32, 36

If you love Jesus and live for Him, you will be free of fear and insecurity, for perfect love casts out fear (1 John 4:18).

• **Contentment**

Godliness with contentment is great gain (1 Timothy 6:6). Greed is insatiable; it deprives people of the ability to really enjoy life. Rather than enjoy life, greedy people spend their time, energy, money, etc. trying to satisfy their greed. Unfortunately, the more they try to satisfy their greed, the more it increases. But in Christ you are content at any level you are per time, and enjoy every step of the way.

Life is exciting when Jesus is your Lord and Saviour. Believe in Him and enjoy life through His name.

Chapter Five

Walking With Jesus

Some people consider walking with Jesus a degrading thing to do; an association that would cost them the good things of life and deprive them of their social life and interaction with people that matter in society. The truth is actually the exact opposite. Your association with Christ will only cost you your sins, and nothing more. Walking with Jesus is walking with the creator of the universe, which means walking with the ultimate authority, who can change people and situations to grant you your desires.

I have not had any cause for regrets since I started walking with Jesus. I am in charge of my life and the circumstances around me. As long as I remain in the faith, all things have no choice but to work together for my good. I walk with my head held high, and if I need the services of anybody, the favour of God causes the person to render such services.

It is wisdom to walk with Jesus; it is probably the best decision you will ever make in life.

Is Following Jesus Easy?

Many people are hesitant to surrender fully to Jesus, because they consider following Him as being difficult. Their belief stems from seeing some other believers think and behave so. Is following Jesus really a difficult thing?

> *Come to Me, all you who labor and are heavy laden, and I will give you rest. Take My yoke upon you and learn from Me, for I am gentle and lowly in heart, and you will find rest for your souls. For My yoke is easy and My burden is light."*

> Matthew 11:28-30

To the contrary, Jesus said His yoke is easy and His burden light. "Easier said than done," I can hear some saying in their minds. But Jesus always says what He means and means what He says, so we must believe whatever He tells us. Numbers

23:19 tells us that, *"God is not a man, that he should lie; neither the son of man, that he should repent: hath he said, and shall he not do it? Or hath he spoken, and shall he not make it good?"* (KJV)

Following Jesus is easy if you are totally surrendered to Him and truly make Him the Lord of your life. Like Jesus advised, learn of Him, and you will find rest for your soul. The problem is that we still believe the wrong teachings and want to do things our own way. When you really get to know Jesus, not just as your Saviour, but also as your Lord and friend, you will discover that Jesus' yoke is easy indeed. Jesus never asks His own to do what is impossible or difficult. He would always make a way out for you if it is beyond you (1 Corinthians 10:13).

When Jesus is your Lord, you do as He says. It's His to call the shots and yours to simply obey. Believing Christians should be like soldiers who do nothing but obey the last command. Soldiers allow their superiors to do all the thinking while

149

they simply carry out their orders. They don't entangle themselves with the affairs of this life; that they may please him who had chosen them to be soldiers (2 Timothy 2:4).

A major challenge some people have in following Jesus is that they don't trust Him enough with their entire lives. They can't trust Him to fully guide and direct the affairs of their lives. While they allow Him to be Lord of some aspects of their lives, they still reserve some areas of their lives where they want absolute control of. But the Bible tells us in Proverbs 3:5-6 to, *"Trust in the Lord with all thine heart; and lean not unto thine own understanding. In all thy ways acknowledge him, and he shall direct thy paths"* (KJV).

For some, the difficult thing when it comes to following Jesus is to sit at His feet and learn of Him. They can't create the time to study the word of God (the Bible) and pray. But the closer your relationship with God, the easier it is to follow Jesus. They that do know their God shall be strong and do exploits (Daniel 11:32).

Jesus' yoke is easy because not only will He teach you what to do, He will also help you accomplish it. He will be with you all the way. He says He will never leave you nor forsake you (Hebrews 13:5). Your part is to totally surrender to Him and obey His word. When you learn to obey God, the Holy Spirit will always lead you by God's word every step of the way. You only have to listen for His instructions. This makes following Jesus easy, as you will always hear a word behind you saying, "This is the way, walk in it" (Isaiah 30:21)

Free yourself from the enemy's bondage that has misled you into thinking that following Jesus is difficult. Jesus loves you and desires to reveal Himself to you. Commit your life to Him, trust Him, and you will discover that His yoke is truly easy.

Is Jesus' Doctrine Worth Following?

"Is it foolishness to follow Jesus' doctrine? Are His words true?" These and many more questions are racing through the minds of some today. Some wonder why some believers in Jesus "waste" their time and resources in preaching the gospel. Some people see them as being foolish, while yet others see them as jobless people.

A man named Paul the apostle has the perfect answers to these questions. Apostle Paul was an unbeliever and a frontline persecutor of the Church of Jesus before he was converted. From Acts 7:58 to 9:2, Paul (who was then known as Saul) was a terror to the Church of Jesus. But he met with Jesus on his way to Damascus, and everything changed. From a persecutor of Christians, Paul became a disciple of Jesus! So he has experienced both sides. What does he think? Is Jesus worth following?

> *For I am the least of the apostles, who am not worthy to be called an apostle, because I persecuted the church of God. But by the grace of God I am what I am, and His grace toward me was not in vain; but I labored more abundantly than they*

all, yet not I, but the grace of God which was with me.

1 Corinthians 15:9-10

I have fought the good fight, I have finished the race, I have kept the faith. Finally, there is laid up for me the crown of righteousness, which the Lord, the righteous Judge, will give to me on that Day, and not to me only but also to all who have loved His appearing.

2 Timothy 4:7-8

For to me, to live is Christ, and to die is gain. But if I live on in the flesh, this will mean fruit from my labor; yet what I shall choose I cannot tell. For I am hard-pressed between the two, having a desire to depart and be with Christ, which is far better.

Philippians 1:21-23

Paul couldn't have enough of Jesus and His gospel! He increased in the knowledge of Christ and became a great apostle of Jesus, to the point that he laboured more than the other apostles, though he was the last to be converted (1 Corinthians 15:9-10). He wrote half of the New Testaments books based on the revelations he got from Christ Himself (Galatians 1:11-12).

Paul suffered so much for the name and gospel of Jesus (2 Corinthians 11:22-33), but it was nothing to him (Philippians 3:7-8). For him, to continue living is to continue living for Christ and to die would be gain, since he would depart to be with Christ, which he considered as being far better (Philippians 1:21-23). In his last letter to Timothy, Paul considered his journey as a believing Christian a good fight, and was glad he finished the race and kept the faith till the end, now waiting for the promised crown of righteousness (2 Timothy 4:7-8).

Paul, a man who was earlier against the doctrines of Christ, later became one that preached it with so much tenacity, not minding the persecutions. He must have discovered that there is truly no other name under heaven by which man can be saved, except through the name of Jesus (Acts 4:12).

His knowledge of Christ was so deep and profound, and the miracles, signs and wonders God did through him were also equally great (Acts 19:11-17). His revelations of Christ made him a god over death. Many attempts to kill him failed; he was rather the one who decided whether to stay and help the brethren or to depart and be with Christ (Philippians 1:21-24). He died only after his assignment on earth was completed. That is the best way to go!

So when people ask, "What if we get to heaven and discover the doctrines of Christ are not true?" I would always reply them, "What if we get to heaven and they are all true?" You lose nothing following Jesus Christ except the pleasures of sin. Take everything from a believing Christian and leave him with only Jesus; and you will discover that you have taken nothing away from him. This is because Christ is able to restore to him all that was lost. Even if they are not fully restored here on earth, he would still enjoy eternal life with Jesus. The three Hebrew boys in Daniel could care less about being thrown into the fiery furnace. And rather than dying, they lived and were promoted!

Is the doctrine of Jesus worth following? Let's find out from a unique set of people in Jesus' days.

Jesus' Women

God created women to be helpers fit for the various needs of men (Genesis 2:18). Jesus' women were indeed help meets in His ministry. These women's role and contributions to His ministry enabled Him to fulfill His assignment on the earth.

Jesus' coming to the earth started with a woman - Mary. She was a virgin and strong believer in God's words. She believed in a seeming impossible feat by man's standard and was used by God to birth His plan for man's redemption. Not much was said about Joseph her husband, but Mary was fully involved in Jesus' ministry. She initiated His first miracle (the turning of water into wine) at the wedding in Cana of Galilee (John 2:1-11), and was always around Him, even at His death.

Jesus' women ministered to His needs. Though Jesus was anointed, He still had physical needs which needed to be met, to be able to operate on earth. The women provided His food, and I believe His clothing as well, out of what they had. They served Jesus with their money.

> *And certain women who had been healed of evil spirits and infirmities—Mary called Magdalene, out of whom had come seven demons, and Joanna the wife of Chuza, Herod's steward, and Susanna, and many others who provided for Him from their substance.*
>
> Luke 8:2-3

Jesus had earlier healed some of these women, who later became His followers and showed their appreciation by ministering to His needs. One of

157

such woman broke a precious alabaster box of ointment and poured it on His feet and wiped them with her hair, preparatory to His death and burial (Mark 14:3-9). Two of these women, Mary Magdalene and Mary the mother of Joses, followed Jesus' body to where it was laid (Mark 15:47).

On resurrection day, these same women, along with some others, went to anoint His body at the tomb and were the first to discover that He had risen as He had said (Luke 24:1-10). Mary Magdalene was the first person Jesus appeared to after His resurrection. She became the first person to spread the good news that Jesus was alive (Mark 16:9-10)!

What do all these women have in common? They believed in Jesus Christ and His ministry, and so became His faithful followers. They served Him with their means, time and energy; they were always there for Him. They were ever grateful and thankful to Jesus Christ for their salvation and healing.

Some people claim to be Christians, but are too busy to serve God. Some others do not consider serving God with their money, time and energy as part of their Christian walk with Him. But God is still looking for men and women who are willing and available to be used in fulfilling His plan and purpose for man. The contributions of these women in Jesus' ministry were written for us to learn and do likewise. Women are still playing important roles in the ministry of the gospel of our Lord Jesus today. The question is: "What is your role and contribution to the gospel?" It doesn't matter whether you are a man or a woman.

What to Live For On Earth

What are you living for? What is it in your life today that when it ends your life too will come to an end? People live for different reasons, and some have lived for reasons that have made their lives miserable and have even destroyed them in their prime.

But there is what to live that can make your life both enjoyable and fulfilling. You can enjoy a fruitful and long life when you live for the right reason. Living for a good cause can make you declare boldly like Apostle Paul:

> *For to me to live is Christ, and to die is gain.*

Philippians 1:21

Taking a walk in my neighbourhood one morning, I took note of a bill board for the first time. On it was written, "We live for superstars," and it had the pictures of three sport stars on it. I wondered how long they could live for them. What if the superstars fall out with the public or die early? What would they now live for?

Unfortunately people choose the wrong thing to live for. Some live for their children, careers, reputation, money, people, etc. That is why they are devastated when something unpleasant and unexpected happens. Some die shortly after such incidences because they can't cope with the loss or shame.

Is there really what to live for in order to enjoy life on earth to the fullest? Yes! Live for something that is durable and will outlive you. The reason should be such that if anything goes wrong, your joy will still be intact. You should be able to share it with others. It should make you desire long life.

You probably are wondering what this might be. The answer is in Philippians 1:21. Jesus Christ is who and what to live for to enjoy a fulfilled life here on earth. When you have Jesus, you have everything: joy, peace, longevity, prosperity, etc. Having Jesus does not reduce you; it instead increases you. Jesus never abandons or forsakes those who live for Him. He came to the earth to give you the abundant life (John 10:10) and unending joy (John 16:24).

Living for Jesus Christ is to live for success and victory. No one who lives for Christ goes unnoticed. As you obey God and walk in line with His word, God lifts you and blesses you. This reminds me of the ass that Jesus rode on on the day of His triumphant entry into Jerusalem. Though people spread their garments on the ground for Jesus to ride on, it was actually the ass that rode on them, as Jesus was seated on the ass (Matthew 21:7-8).

Living a fulfilled life is possible only if we live for Jesus, as He will help you discover what you were created for. The Almighty God dwells in every believer and empowers them to live for Jesus. What you can't do, He supplies the strength and wisdom to carry it out. Jesus Christ is really who and what to live for. He not only enables you to enjoy longevity on earth, but also empowers you to enjoy life after death. You get to enjoy both an abundant life here on earth and also eternal life in heaven!

Chapter Six

Jesus and Celebration

Jesus Christ is very important to the world. Not only does He save people from their sins, He also heals, delivers and restores. In addition, His birth date is widely used to label or number years: Before Christ (BC) and Anno Domini (AD) are designations used for dates before and after Jesus' birth respectively. He is truly no ordinary person! School calendars are also widely programmed to have schools closed during the Christmas and Easter periods. This is to allow people celebrate these landmark events with their loved ones.

Christmas is a season of excitement and celebration. It is also a season of giving and receiving of presents, as shops worldwide are flooded with merchandise ready to be sold specifically during this season. Wrapped gifts and greeting cards are exchanged between families, friends, colleagues and loved ones. So much money is spent buying Christmas trees and decorations to lighten homes, streets and offices. A lot of cooking goes on during the Christmas holidays too.

What really is the essence of Christmas? Why do we celebrate Christmas? I believe people should go beyond the eating, drinking and merry making of the season to understand the essence of the celebration, so they can better tap into the benefits and power they carry.

Christmas and Easter celebrations are very special to me. I will tell you why they are special to me, and hope they will become special to you as well.

For unto us a Child is born, unto us a Son is given; and the government will be upon His shoulder. And His name will be called Wonderful, Counselor, Mighty God, Everlasting Father, Prince of Peace.

Isaiah 9:6

And she will bring forth a Son, and you shall call His name Jesus, for He will save His people from their sins. Matthew 1:21

But one of the elders said to me, "Do not weep. Behold, the Lion of the tribe of Judah, the Root of David, has prevailed to open the scroll and to loose its seven seals."

Revelation 5:5

I believe we got the tradition of giving gifts during Christmas from God the Father, Who gave the world His only begotten Son, Jesus. Christmas is a commemoration of the birth of Jesus Christ. God gave us His best during this season many years ago, which we now mimic by giving presents to others during Christmas.

Unfortunately, however, whereas many love receiving presents at Christmas, very few actually know the child that was born on that precious day, and why it is so important to keep remembering the day He was born, over 2,000 years ago. The Christmas celebration is much more than feasting and visiting loved ones. Jesus was born to save humanity from their sins and the works of Satan that had held them captive (1 John 1:7; 1 John

165

3:8). He is the Saviour of the whole world. There is no other name by which man can be saved but the name of Jesus (Acts 4:12).

God so love you and me, that He sent His only child Jesus to the world, that whosoever believes in Him will not perish, but have eternal life (John 3:16). Jesus came to bridge the gap between God and man, and to restore the original relationship they both had in the Garden of Eden (2 Corinthians 5:18-19). He came to restore all that man lost when Adam sold out to the devil, and to cause all who believe in Him to reign in life (Romans 5:7-8).

Though He is the King of kings, Jesus refused to be made an earthly king. He departed from their midst when the Jews tried to make Him a king, because that was not part of His assignment (John 6:15). He was a man on a mission. Jesus came to the earth with a specific mission from God, and returned to the Father when His assignment was done. His mission included His death on the cross for the sins of the whole world. As a result, as many as believe in Him and call upon Him shall be saved!

Knowing that Jesus' birth would be his end, Satan the enemy tried to kill Him as a child (Matthew 2:13-16; Revelations 12:4-5). That is why Christians celebrate Christmas. It symbolises our victory over the enemy through Christ. Just as prophesied by Simeon, the birth of Jesus is for the falling of your enemy and strongholds, but for your rising (Luke 2:34). Therefore, remind yourself that your Redeemer came to redeem you from the curse of the law, connecting you back to all the blessings of Abraham (Galatians 3:13-14).

For me, Christmas is truly a time to rejoice and make merry, because God's chosen vessel for the redemption of humanity was born! You and I are free in Christ if we receive Him as our Saviour. That is why we rejoice and are glad. Jesus is called Wonderful because He is full of wonders. Even after His death on the cross, Jesus' name is still doing wonders today. He is also the Great Counsellor, our Mighty God, and the Prince of peace. Not only does He give peace to our souls, He also brings peace between the believer and God.

Those who saw the first Christmas rejoiced greatly at witnessing it (the shepherds and wise men from the East). We should do likewise. Simeon was so thankful to God for the opportunity of seeing Jesus!

> *For my eyes have seen Your salvation which You have prepared before the face of all peoples, a light to bring revelation to the Gentiles, and the glory of Your people Israel.*
>
> Luke 2:30-32

Another reason I rejoice at Christmas is because of the fulfilment of prophecies. Right from Genesis, the entire Old Testament is replete with prophecies of the birth of Jesus. The birth of Jesus is a proof that God keeps His promises; a proof that He does what He says. Therefore, you can trust Him to perform whatever promise He has made to you.

The Christmas season should be a time to evaluate our walk with God and take concrete steps towards fulfilling the true essence of Christmas in our lives. Have you accepted God's salvation? Is Jesus' glory evident in your life? As you go about visiting loved ones and enjoying the holiday, be sure to be in God's presence also.

The Power of His Resurrection

Another very important celebration in Christendom and the world is Easter. It is a time Christians celebrate the death, burial and resurrection of Jesus from the dead. Jesus died a shameful death on the cross so He can pay the price in full for man's sins. He was buried, but rose from the dead three days later, and is now seated at the right hand of God in heaven.

> *I am He who lives, and was dead, and behold, I am alive forevermore. Amen. And I have the keys of Hades and of Death.*
>
> Revelation 1:18

Jesus' resurrection from the dead is the anchor of the Christian faith. The purpose of Jesus coming to the earth and dying on the cross would have been incomplete if He had not risen from the dead. Our victory over sin and Satan lies in Jesus' death and resurrection. This wisdom of God (which seemed like foolishness at the time) totally defeated the enemy.

> *But we speak the wisdom of God in a mystery, the hidden wisdom which God ordained before the ages for our glory, which none of the rulers of this age knew; for had they known, they would not have crucified the Lord of glory.*

1 Corinthians 2:7-8

The resurrection of Jesus reconciled us back to God (1 Peter 1:3) and restored man back to the position and relationship He had with God in the Garden of Eden, before the fall. This is why Christians celebrate Easter. A revelation of this truth and benefits would cause you to celebrate Easter daily.

Jesus' work of redemption is finished! The long lasting effects of this victory belong to all that accept Jesus Christ as their personal Lord and Saviour. The celebration at Easter is simply our acknowledgement and appreciation of what Jesus suffered and achieved for man. It is also a reminder and celebration of the devil's defeat forever. The devil lost all the power he had over Christians the day Jesus rose from the dead (Hebrews 2:14). An understanding of the devil's total defeat empowers Christians to challenge the enemy and exercise their authority over him in Jesus name.

In addition to the victory over the devil and sin, there is also the unlimited power made available to believers through the resurrection of Jesus from the dead. This power is a very great, howbeit untapped blessing of the Easter celebration. Easter Sunday should not only remind us of our salvation in Christ, but also the resurrection power that is at work in us and for us.

That I may know Him and the power of His resurrection, and the fellowship of His sufferings, being conformed to His death.

Philippians 3:10

That if possible I may attain to the [spiritual and moral] resurrection [that lifts me] out from among the dead [even while in the body].

– Philippians 3:11 (AMP)

And [so that you can know and understand] what is the immeasurable and unlimited and surpassing greatness of His power in and for us who believe, as demonstrated in the working of His mighty strength,

Which He exerted in Christ when He raised Him from the dead and seated

Him at His [own] right hand in the heavenly [places].

– Ephesians 1:19-20 (AMP)

But if the Spirit of Him who raised Jesus from the dead dwells in you, He who raised Christ from the dead will also give life to your mortal bodies through His Spirit who dwells in you.

– Romans 8:11

Every believer needs to know the immeasurable, unlimited and surpassing greatness of God's resurrection power that is at work in and for them. Salvation gives us access to this incredible power by the in-dwelling of the Holy Spirit. Some blessings we enjoy through the resurrection power include:

- **Dead and Sleeping Anointing Awakened**

  The resurrection power is able to revive your spiritual life. If, for example, your hitherto vibrant Christian walk is down to a point where you are now struggling, the resurrection power can help get you back on track. The working of His mighty power will not only restore your spiritual life, but will take it to a higher level of glory. So reach out for the power of His resurrection now.

- **Empower Your Moral Life**

  The resurrection power will enable you live right before God. It does this by breaking habits that had ensnared you in the past, and instead empower you to build new and healthy habits.

- **Raises Dead Or Dying Things**

  The resurrection power raises everything dying or dead within or around you. Such things might include your health, business, marriage or ministry. God who raised Jesus from the dead will raise any of these by His Spirit that dwells in the believer. All they need do is to invoke by faith the power of His resurrection on that issue, and it will come alive again (Romans 8:11).

- **Causes Multiplication**

  The resurrection of Jesus empowers believers to do more works than Jesus did. The new birth grants every believer the privilege to enjoy all-round multiplication. Jesus' mighty power within them through the in-dwelling Holy Spirit empowers them to do in greater measure the works that Jesus did and whatever they can imagine Him do (John 14:12).

- **Destroys Every Siege**

  The resurrection power can also destroy whatever evil siege that had been laid against your life and destiny, no matter how long they have buffeted you. The power of His resurrection is the tool with which God destroys every siege against your financial breakthrough, healing, academic excellence, ministry success, fruitfulness, spiritual life and blessings, etc.

Note, however, that a Christian who lacks an understanding of Jesus' death and resurrection will still be molested and oppressed by the enemy. That is why Satan will do everything possible to stop the preaching and teaching of the resurrection of Jesus and its power. Easter is definitely one day that Jesus' resurrection is preached all over the world. Until this truth is preached, people will not believe or be delivered (Romans 10:14).

Easter should, therefore, mean more than eating and drinking. It is a day to praise God and thank Him for His great wisdom of salvation. This attitude provokes God's blessings and the manifestation of the resurrection power of Jesus Christ.

The Best Easter Gift

The Easter season is when Christians celebrate their freedom from Satan's oppression. Believers are remind that they have been set free from the enemy's authority by Jesus' rising from the dead; and are now able to take back all that he had stolen from them. This victory is truly worth celebrating. Some people give gifts during this season. What do you think is the best gift to give or receive during Easter?

...But also for us. It shall be imputed to us who believe in Him who raised up Jesus our Lord from the dead, who was delivered up because of our offenses, and was raised because of our justification.

Romans 4:24-25

Christ has redeemed us from the curse of the law, having become a curse for us (for it is written, "Cursed is everyone who hangs on a tree"), that the blessing of Abraham might come upon the Gentiles in Christ Jesus, that we might receive the promise of the Spirit through faith.

Galatians 3:13-14

But to those who are called, both Jews and Greeks, Christ the power of God and the wisdom of God.

1 Corinthians 1:24

Jesus is the best gift to give or receive, especially during the Easter season. You need to receive Jesus as Lord and Saviour if you have not done so yet. If you have, you need to spread the joy around by telling someone else of their need for Jesus.

Jesus Christ fully paid the price for whatever we may have owed the enemy by hanging on the cross in our place. His shed blood on the cross of Calvary washes clean everyone who dares to believe and appropriate it. They receive His righteousness, and are then filled with peace and joy in the Holy Ghost (2 Corinthians 5:17-21). This is the perfect gift for all seasons.

Jesus is the answer to the world's many bugging issues today. He gives victory, peace, direction, wisdom and power, healing, prosperity, to mention just a few. He is the answer to that challenge confronting you right now. Receive Him into your life today as Lord and Saviour, and see the difference He makes in people's lives. After He has transformed your life, tell others about Him; they will ever be grateful that you did.

Therefore, while others are looking for Easter presents to buy, look for whom to give this perfect gift to. The good news is that it is free! Freely have you received Him, freely you are commanded to give. Salvation is for everybody, including that horrible neighbour of yours. Jesus will turn him into the best neighbour ever if you show him the way. "What if they reject this free gift?" you may ask. Let that not bother you. Just share the love of Jesus with the person and leave the job of conviction to the Holy Spirit. Your duty is to sow the seed of the word, which may yield fruits immediately or later.

Chapter Seven

You and Jesus

I believe you now have a better understanding of who Jesus Christ is. I also expect that if before reading this book you didn't know Him you should by now, and have decided to entrust your life to Him. That is the best decision you will ever make.

I will never trade my relationship with Jesus Christ for anything else. There is nothing better out there. My connection to Him gives me all I need here on earth and assures me of security here after. I have the kind of peace that nothing else can give; money can't buy this kind of peace. I also have joy that is not dependent on what I have or don't have. I'm truly satisfied with Jesus!

If you haven't made that great decision yet, I hope you will as you read this concluding chapter. Let me show you how you can relate with Jesus personally.

You Have a Friend in Jesus

Are you a friend of Jesus? Do you know what it means to have a friend in Jesus? Being without friends is lonely and frustrating, and it's worse when Jesus is not your friend. Jesus wants to be friends with all; unfortunately, however, only those who accept Him really get to be His friend.

Jesus is the friend you need at all times; whether in times of joy and peace or in times of sorrow and disappointments. He is always there for His friends. You don't need to travel far to reach Him, neither do you need to spend money calling Him. He is ever present and can be there with you right away.

Having a friend in Jesus is to have peace of mind in times of trouble. He comforts us and leads us in the path of peace and joy (Psalm 23:2). Have you ever needed a shoulder to cry on? Jesus' shoulders are ever available. Yes, you can pour your heart out to Him, for He truly understands and cares about all that concerns you.

For we do not have a High Priest Who is unable to understand and sympathize and have a shared feeling with our weakness and infirmities and liability to the assaults of temptation, but One Who has been tempted in every respect as we, yet without sinning.

Hebrews 4:15 (AMP)

"A good friend can tell what the matter with you is in a minute. He may not seem such a good friend after telling," says Arthur Brisbane. Jesus is a friend indeed! He tells you when you are wrong. In fact, He rebukes and chastens His friends; all because He loves them and does not want them to go down the road of destruction (Hebrews 12:6).

Jesus is also a very humorous friend. He amuses and makes people laugh. He can make you smile even in between your tears. What love! Having Jesus as your friend means being excited all the time, as there is always something to look forward to. Though others may desert you, Jesus would never. You will never be lonely if Jesus is your friend.

O how I love Jesus and desire to know Him more and more! I desire to know and enjoy the wisdom of His friendship; a friendship I will give anything for, and never trade for anything else. It is so sweet to walk with Jesus and behold the beauty of His loveliness and holiness, to follow His directions and experience no failure.

Jesus is a friend of those who do His commands. He calls them friends and not servants (John 15:15). Obedience to God's words qualifies you to be a friend of Jesus. It is a relationship you will never regret, as it is a friendship full of blessings, peace and joy. Make Jesus your friend today and experience what it means to have a friend in Jesus.

You Need To Know Jesus

You may be asking, "Why do I need to know Jesus more?" It is not enough to just be saved and go to church. On the contrary, life in Christ is much more than that. It is a relationship that must be nurtured and developed both for earthly and eternal benefits.

Take My yoke upon you and learn of Me, for I am gentle (meek) and humble (lowly) in heart, and you will find rest (relief and ease and refreshment and recreation and blessed quiet) for your souls.

Matthew 11:29 (AMP)

The thief does not come except to steal, and to kill, and to destroy. I have come that they may have life, and that they may have it more abundantly.

John 10:10

To know Jesus Christ is to know God and your inheritance in Him. A life without Christ is a life full of crisis. Therefore, a better knowledge of Jesus keeps you farther away from crisis. In Him you live, and move and have your being.

A close relationship with the Lord is sweet! There is so much joy and peace, contentment and liberty in Christ. If you get to know Jesus more you will not trade your relationship with Him for anything else, including money. You would want to be with Him all the time. When you know how much He loves you, you would want to love Him back. So, join me and taste, and see that the Lord is good.

Each new day with Jesus is sweeter than the previous day. You will love Him more and more as you abide in Him. He will also reveal more of Himself to you as you walk with Him. You will go beyond seeing Him merely as your Saviour, to seeing Him as your best friend, comforter, and present help in times of need. Also, the more you know Jesus, the more you will appreciate the meanings of all His names, because you will see them manifesting in your life. For instance, you will truly experience Him as your healer and provider, because He will always heal you and provide for all your needs.

Knowing Jesus will grant you more access to all of God's blessings. Jesus is the access to all that God the Father has to offer, including eternal life. God

186

has designed it in such a way that you will get nothing from Him except when you ask in the name of Jesus (John 14:13-14; 15:16; 16:23-24). To exercise your dominion on earth and fully enjoy all that salvation has to offer, you need to have a deeper knowledge and relationship with Jesus.

Most importantly, Jesus desires to have a closer relationship with you. He wants you to fully enjoy and utilize the power He purchased with His blood for you. But He can only teach you how to do so when you draw closer to Him.

It pays to know Jesus better; it is never a wasted exercise. I will give anything to have a closer walk with Him. I enjoy unending peace because of Jesus. I am not afraid of tomorrow because I know He will always be there for me. I may not be sure of many things, but I am certainly sure of His love for me. His love has kept me through thick and thin. Truly Jesus is everything to me. The good news is that you too can have that kind of relationship with Him.

A Closer Walk with Jesus

Seeking a closer relationship with Jesus is a huge step towards a more glorious life that is full of peace, victory and blessings.

> *That I may know Him and the power of His resurrection, and the fellowship of His sufferings, being conformed to His death,*
>
> Philippians 3:10

> *But the Helper, the Holy Spirit, whom the Father will send in My name, <u>He will teach you all things,</u> and bring to your remembrance all things that I said to you.*
>
> John 14:26

The deeper you know Christ, the farther away from crises you get. Also, since Jesus is the way to God the Father, the closer you are to Him the more access you have to God's blessings. Therefore, learning how to know Christ more is a wise thing to do. Let me show you some ways of achieving this.

- **Have an open heart**

  Now a certain woman named Lydia heard us. She was a seller of purple from the city of Thyatira, who worshiped God. The Lord opened her heart to heed the things spoken by Paul.

  Acts 16:14

Ask God to give you an open heart to learn more about the Lord. It will be difficult for a mind clogged with philosophy and traditions of men to know the Lord more. Therefore, there is a need to have an open mind towards the gospel of Jesus so He can truly reveal Himself to you.

- **Ask for the help of the Holy Spirit**

  He will glorify Me, for He will take of what is Mine and declare it to you.

  John 16:14

The Holy Spirit is there to reveal Christ to you, so engage His help. He is the most authentic person to consult about Jesus. Simply ask Him to teach you more about Jesus and expect Him to do just that.

- **Study the Bible**

  In the beginning was the Word, and the Word was with God, and the Word was God.

  And the Word became flesh and dwelt among us, and we beheld His glory, the glory as of the only begotten of the Father, full of grace and truth.

  John 1:1, 14

If you want to know more about a person, you must read about that person. Likewise, if you want to know more about Jesus, you need to read and study the Bible. The Bible is the word of God, and Jesus is the word of God. The scriptures from Genesis to Revelation are centred on Jesus Christ. The word of God is also Spirit and life; therefore, your life is imparted as you read the Bible. No man or written materials can tell you about Christ better than the Bible. So, as you read and study the Bible with the help of the Holy Spirit, the word of God will become flesh to you. You will know and

190

understand Jesus more, as well as be able to apply the Bible to your daily life and affairs.

- **Pray**

  [For I always pray to] the God of our Lord Jesus Christ, the Father of glory, that He may grant you a spirit of wisdom and revelation [of insight into mysteries and secrets] in the [deep and intimate] knowledge of him.

  Ephesians 1:17 (AMP)

The more time you spend with an individual, the better you get to know him or her. In like manner, the more time you spend fellowshipping with God in prayer, the better you will get to know Jesus. This is because you can't get to the Father except through Jesus. We pray in the name of Jesus, and our fellowship is with God the Father, Jesus Christ (the Son) and the Holy Spirit.

- **Be full of thanks and praises**

  Enter into His gates with thanksgiving, and into His courts

with praise, be thankful to Him, and
bless His name.

You can't learn much about Jesus without a heart of gratitude. This is because God inhabits the praises of His people. Jesus is naturally attracted to someone with a heart full of praises and thanksgiving, and He would usually reveal Himself to the person when He comes. Praise provokes revelations from God, including revelations about Jesus.

- **Be obedient**

  The person who has my commands and keeps them is the one who [really] loves Me; and whoever [really] loves Me will be loved by My Father, and I [too] will love him and will show (reveal, manifest) Myself to him. [I will let Myself be clearly seen by him and make Myself real to him.]

  John 14:21 (AMP)

Obedience opens you up to a deeper knowledge of Jesus, as He reveals Himself only to those who obey His commands. This is probably the cheapest way of getting to know Jesus more. Jesus said He would make Himself be clearly seen, and make Himself real to the one who obeys Him.

- **Be open for correction**

    For whom the Lord loves He chastens, and scourges every son whom He receives."

    For they indeed for a few days chastened us as seemed best to them, but He for our profit, that we may be partakers of His holiness.

    Hebrews 12:6, 10

When you are not open to corrections from Jesus you cut yourself off from Him revealing Himself to you and showing you things. The Lord uses corrections to deliver us from the evil one. Therefore, anyone that hates correction cannot enjoy a closer relationship with the Lord, and is headed for disaster.

You can get to know Jesus more and have Him reveal Himself to you by doing the things I listed above. Remember that they that do know their God shall be strong and shall do exploits (Daniel 11:32).

Finding Jesus

Have you made Jesus your Lord and Saviour yet? What is still keeping you? It is important that everyone finds Jesus. He's right there waiting for you; just a cry away from you! He said of Himself:

> *Behold, I stand at the door and knock. If anyone hears My voice and opens the door, I will come in to him and dine with him, and he with Me.*
>
> Revelations 3:20

Simply open the door of your heart to Him right now and that will be the best decision you have ever made. Doing this is very simple. The Bible shows us how.

> *If you declare with your mouth, "Jesus is Lord," and believe in your*

heart that God raised him from the dead, you will be saved. For it is with your heart that you believe and are justified, and it is with your mouth that you profess your faith and are saved.

Romans 10:9-10 (NIV)

But go and learn what this means: 'I desire mercy and not sacrifice.' For I did not come to call the righteous, but sinners, to repentance."

Matthew 9:13

All that the Father gives Me will come to Me, and the one who comes to Me I will by no means cast out.

John 6:37

Everyone, including you, needs to find Jesus, because He is the only way and access to God and all His blessings (John 14:6). There is another urgent reason people need to find Jesus: the world is fast coming to an end, and there will be no mercy once the door of heaven is closed. Jesus is already at the door of your heart knocking, asking you to open up for Him to come into your life. So, open up now!

Is there any special way of opening up to Jesus? No. Come just as you are to Him. He came to call sinners to repentance, so will not turn anyone that comes to Him away, no matter how sinful.

> *"Come now, and let us reason together,"*
> *says the LORD, "Though your sins are like scarlet, they shall be as white as snow; though they are red like crimson, they shall be as wool.*

> Isaiah 1:18

The Bible tells us that we all have sinned and fallen short of God's glory (Romans 3:23). Our righteousness is like filthy rags before God (Isaiah 64:6). As a result, we all need a Saviour. Jesus is that Saviour; the only way to God, and God's only provision for our salvation. He is the only One that can save us from our sins and certain death and destruction.

For God so loved the world that He gave His only begotten Son, that whoever believes in Him should not perish but have everlasting life.

John 3:16

To find Jesus and His peace, you must ask Him to come into your heart; you must declare with your mouth that "Jesus is Lord," and believe in your heart that God raised him from the dead. Only after doing these can you truly find Jesus. It is with our hearts that we believe and are justified, and with our mouth that we profess our faith and are saved. It is this simple because the gospel of our Lord Jesus Christ is not complicated.

Pray this simple prayer of faith to invite Jesus into your heart, and make Him Lord of your life:

Lord Jesus, I come to You today. I am a sinner, I cannot help myself. Wash me with Your blood. I believe You died for me and rose again on the third day for my justification. I confess You as my

personal Lord and Saviour. Father, I thank You for saving me. I am born again, saved, delivered and healed, in Jesus name!

Amen!

Congratulations and welcome to the family of God! You are now born again; you are now a child of God, and Jesus is your Saviour. To grow as every child needs to, build upon this foundation of salvation through prayers, study of the Bible and fellowship with other believing Christians in Bible-believing churches and fellowships. As you study the word of God and pray more, you will learn more about Jesus and be closer drawn to Him. You will also learn how to live in this new kingdom that you have been born into.

Marketing Jesus

Do you really love Jesus? Why then is it difficult for you to market Him or tell others about Him? Should you be ashamed of the one you love? Can you tell others about your lover? Then why is it so difficult to tell others about Jesus? Some will tell of how they cannot live without their lovers, and would gladly tell others about them. They are not shy telling others about their lover. But this same person would be shy speaking about Jesus and His great benefits to mankind!

We are commanded to tell others about Jesus. He wasn't ashamed of us; we shouldn't be of Him. If we love Him and truly believe that the world needs Him to save them, then we must be bold and purposeful in making Him known to the world.

> *Go therefore and make disciples of all the nations, baptizing them in the name of the Father and of the Son and of the Holy Spirit, teaching them to observe all things that I have commanded you; and lo, I am with you always, even to the end of the age."*

Matthew 28:19-20

A lady said something very profound to me one day. I was trying to market a particular product to her, and she said to me, "If all Christian marketers would market Christ the way they market this product and other network marketing products, this world would be a changed place." It got me thinking and wondering how and why we could boldly and shamelessly market many other things except the One we profess to love. Why is it so difficult?

People are able to easily market these other things and people for money, because they need to eat, clothe their bodies, take care of their families and pay their bills. I agree that marketing Jesus doesn't immediately put money in their pockets. But if you truly love God you will obey His commandments (John 14:15), and one of His commandments is that we should go and make disciples of all nations, and teach them to observe all that He has commanded.

If you can market anything, even if it is to simply recommend a product to someone else, then you should be able to tell someone else about Jesus. You market Jesus by simply telling others about what He has done in your life. Your testimony is enough for the Holy Spirit to work with in saving that lost soul. Remember, you are not the one going to redeem him. You are required to simply do your part and leave the Holy Spirit to do the rest.

It is not enough to sing about how you love Jesus, you need to go a step further and tell others about Him. Will it make any difference? Sure it will. The result may not be instant, but at least a seed has been sown, which will soon bring forth.

Market Jesus, for He is the wisdom and power of God (1 Corinthians 1:24) and the way, the truth and the life (John 14:6). Jesus is the only name by which man can be saved (Acts 4:12). Besides, what joy will fill your heart when you get to heaven and see those you witnessed to there too!

Jesus showed us an example of how to sell the one we love in a difficult market place. The Bible tells us:

> *Looking unto Jesus, the author and*
> *finisher of our faith, who for the joy*

that was set before Him endured the
cross, despising the shame, and has
sat down at the right hand of the
throne of God.

Hebrews 12:2

Jesus, for the joy of seeing all those who would be saved by His sacrifice on the cross, endued the shame of the cross. For the love He had for His Father, Who desired mankind saved and not condemned, Jesus endured the cross, despising the shame. He sacrificed Himself for humanity. We too should emulate Him. We should be moved to tell others about Jesus when we consider all that would perish if they do not hear about Jesus and make Him the Lord of their lives.

The good news is that the grace to follow in Jesus' footsteps by telling others of His saving grace is available, if we desire it. I believe God for this grace upon me, not only for a short time, but for the rest of my life, to boldly and shamelessly market Him to as many people as possible. What about you?

The Life Truth

Are you ready for what must surely come? We are ever consciously or unconsciously preparing for good or bad. That we will all indeed leave this earth one day is a life truth. But the question is, "how ready are you?"

> *Catch us the foxes, the little foxes that spoil the vines, for our vines have tender grapes.*
>
> SOS 2:15

> *"Again, when a righteous man turns from his righteousness and commits iniquity, and I lay a stumbling block before him, he shall die; because you did not give him warning, he shall die in his sin, and <u>his righteousness which he has done shall not be remembered</u>; but his blood I will require at your hand.*
>
> Ezekiel 3:20 (Emphasis mine)

Sometime ago, without planning to, I watched in one week two programmes that talked about people's readiness for eternity. It got my mind racing; I had to examine and re-examine myself.

In one of the stories, a pastor died and had the privilege of seeing both heaven and hell. At the end, the angel that walked with him told him that if he hadn't asked for God's mercy and forgiveness before dying, hell would have been his lot. But the pastor tried to argue with the angel, claiming that as a pastor he had preached about heaven and hell to others. But the angel reminded him of the argument he had with his wife before his accident for which he had not forgiven her.

The life truth is that many may not have a last minute opportunity of asking for forgiveness before dying like the pastor did. Something as simple as unforgiveness can cost you your place in heaven. Though the pastor might have been ready before the quarrel with his wife, his last minute disobedience could have cost him a place in heaven. How ready are you?

The second account was a movie in which the princess (the righteous) felt that the prince (Jesus)

204

was taking His time in coming back, and may not fulfil His promise of returning to take her to His palace. As a result, she decided to go and enjoy herself in the world. Unfortunately, the prince returned shortly after and found her already defiled. The prince left her and returned back to His kingdom, because no defiled person has a place in his kingdom.

The life truth is that Jesus will surely come back to take the saints home. How ready are you for His return? You may have heard people mock the preaching of the return of Jesus. They say this message and warning has been for ages, and has not happened yet. Whether people believe it or not, God's word and plan cannot be changed: Jesus is coming soon. The handwriting is on the wall, for those who would see and understand.

There will be surprises on the last day, as God's word has foretold us in Matthew 7:21-22. What might make a believer miss heaven may not be a "big sin". In most cases, the culprits are the "little foxes" such as unforgiveness, bitterness, the love of money, comparison with others, fornication, envy, jealousy, anger, etc.

There is no big or small sin; sin is sin, no matter how big or little or who commits it. The life truth is that no one knows when Jesus will return, that is why we need to live ready always. Jesus already said His return will be at an unexpected time which only the Father knows (Matthew 24:36-44). He could also return like a thief in the night (1 Thessalonians 5:2). How ready are you for His return? We should be prepared and live everyday expecting Him to come at any moment. This attitude will certainly save us from falling into temptation like the lady in the second story.

Nobody or anything is worth our going to hell. Heaven is real, and hell is real too! If some people ask you, "How sure are you that there is hell?" your reply to them should simply be, "What if there is?" I'd rather live for Christ now and discover later that there is no hell (of course, hell is real) than to live an unrighteous life and find out later that there is hell.

Are you ready for the return of the Prince? What judgment are you expecting to receive from the Almighty? Not ready yet? Praise God that you can still make amends right this minute. Take advantage of it and be ready to meet the Lord. If you are ready to meet your Saviour, praise God! See you there soon!

www.ingramcontent.com/pod-product-compliance
Lightning Source LLC
Chambersburg PA
CBHW032117040426
42449CB00005B/173